Pra

Alone Together

"These poignant stories will ensure readers see Latin America through new eyes as they challenge conventional stereotypes of women traveling alone. They will laugh and cry and relive their own experiences. As one writer states, "we cannot choose where we are born, [but] we can choose where we leave our hearts." For these writers, that place is Latin America."

— **Jill Gibian**, editor of *Argentina: A Traveler's Literary Companion*

"Whether you're into edgy travel tales, searching for the impetus to kick-start your own trip, or simply looking for a gripping read, *Alone Together* is the book for you."

— **Diane Esguerra**, author of *Junkie Buddha: A Journey of Discovery in Peru*

"Finally we have *Alone Together*, a remarkable anthology written by women of many voices and experiences. Every story ensures the reader will feel part of the adventure. Inspiring as well as powerful, this book is a must for all travelers to the region."

— **Marjorie Ag**   *erfly Hill* and winner
              of th**   Honor for Lifetime
                                                            Achievement

"Imbued   vivid description,
and enc   pelling,
and who

"A terrific collection of characterful, colourful vignettes, *Alone Together* ditches the gringo trail in favour of everyday encounters from across Latin America. Often poignant, always personal, it captures what's best about independent travel – the excitement, the fears, the surprises and, above all, the richness of shared humanity. A joy to read."

– **Oliver Balch**, author of *Viva South America! A Journey through a Restless Continent*, shortlisted for Book of the Year by the British Travel Press Awards

"It was fascinating to see the continent from a woman's perspective; I suspect that while most male travellers intellectually understand that there are differences in the challenges we face, many of us don't really understand. *Alone Together* gave me a new, more nuanced perspective. I thoroughly enjoyed it."

– **James Brooman**, author of *North to South: A Man, A Bear and a Bicycle*

"*Alone Together* is the perfect narrative of what it means to discover who you are through your journey. The final page will leave beginner and seasoned travelers with just one question, 'Where should I go next?'"

– **Jennifer Poe**, author of *Hola, Morocha! A Black Woman's Adventures in Buenos Aires: Culture Shock*

"It's refreshing to read *Alone Together*. These writers are so different in the way they tell their stories; how they see the world, what they are seeking. Readers are guaranteed to find a little of their own selves amongst these pages too."

– **Tracy Ashworth**, author of *60 Ways to Die in South America: A Novel about Love, Llamas and trying not to Die*

Alone Together

Tales of Sisterhood and Solitude in Latin America

Edited by

Karen Attman, Victoria Kellaway and Emma Newbery

BOGOTÁ INTERNATIONAL PRESS

Alone Together - Tales of Sisterhood and Solitude in Latin America

ISBN: 978-958-56262-1-8

Published by Bogotá International Press
www.bogotainternationalpress.com
editor@bogotainternationalpress.com

Cover illustration by Alejandro Acosta

Find out more about women's travels in Latin America at:
www.WomenTravelLatinAmerica.com

For every woman who has ever listened... and done it anyway.

Alone Together

Contents

Foreword by Hilary Bradt

Prologue by Amy Baker

Breaking in the Shoes of a Braver Woman
Elizabeth O'Donnell
Is it finally time to start listening to your mother?
Page 23

A Sticky Revelation • Teresa Bruce
The best choices are made at the worst moments
Page 29

Home is a Loaded Word • Elizabeth Holli Wood
The past is a foreign country until it knocks at your door
Page 35

At the Mercy of Men • Sissi Korhonen
They've only ever got one thing on their minds
Page 41

Journalist: Don't Shoot • Ronnie Lovler
Keep your head down and come back with the story
Page 47

Havana Rewind • Courtenay Strickland

If music be the food of love, play on

Page 57

It Has to be Now • Nuria Elkout

There's only one thing less reliable than a chicken bus

Page 61

Missing • Rebecca Hoffmann

Nightmares happen on otherwise ordinary days

Page 65

Could this be the Place? • Julia Buschmann

Childhood dreams only pretend to go away

Page 71

Gunfire in the Night • Kelly Symonds

Wake up, this is happening

Page 81

You're Never Too Old • April Wood

Those itchy feet have a mind of their own

Page 89

The Uninvited Visitor • Allison Yates

With proximity comes great responsibility

Page 93

Look at my Life Now • Rebecca Roach

A real phoenix decides when to emerge

Page 99

A Rugged Kinda Gal • Robin Verwest

Even the best hitchhikers can accept the wrong ride

Page 107

Evening in the Wrong Barrio • Emily Paskevics

They told her to be home by sunset

Page 113

The Painter of Bluefields • Anna Wrochna

Falling in love is the greatest art of all

Page 117

Witness to the Crime • Jade Griffiths

There's no evidence you'll be safer at home

Page 125

The Swim • Caitlin Furio

Has the time come to take the plunge?

Page 127

The Legacy of Berta Cáceres • Gloria Jiménez

The bravest souls refuse to be silenced

Page 137

Gift of Grapes • Kate Rawles

The kindness of strangers may taste the sweetest

Page 143

Just Keep Breathing • Phebe Tempelaars

Alone in the jungle, who is going to save you?

Page 153

We Hadn't Even Said Hello • Paula Veselovschi

Family means no one is forgotten or left behind

Page 159

A Face at the Window • Ailana Navarez

If only you could forget what you weren't meant to see

Page 165

Day One Hundred and Twenty Two • Emma Murray

Some footprints make an impression the tide will never erase

Page 173

The Hangover • Charlotte Mackenzie de Urrea

Beware of the flashbacks that haunt you forever

Page 179

My Polola • Megan Lawton

Can a lone wanderer ever meet her match?

Page 187

Down the Napo River • Stephanie A. Wolcott

Listen to those who have known from the beginning

Page 191

My Shaman • Priyanka Gupta

The spark of modern desire in an ancient land

Page 197

Crossing • Emily Wheeler

Six strangers, one common goal

Page 203

The Clash • Susan Walsh

It can all come down to four familiar punk rockers

Page 209

Incoherent in Copacabana • Camille Mansell

Watch out for vulnerability, it lurks in unlikely shadows

Page 215

Sweet Talkers • Nadia Ho de Guillén

Is it true what they say about Latin lovers?

Page 219

Pointers • Ilona Tonnaer

Those days when you just have to follow the signs

Page 225

Change in Your Pocket • Andrea Jaramillo

The smallest things can make all the difference

Page 233

The Island of Dead Dolls • Fayida Jailler

There's a secret behind every strange obsession

Page 237

But You're a Girl • Megan Benay

In case you hadn't noticed

Page 245

Foreword

I've just returned from the Cheltenham Literature Festival in England where I was speaking about the latest Bradt anthology, *Roam Alone: inspiring tales by reluctant solo travellers*. As I sit down to draft this foreword, I wonder if it's just coincidence that we in Britain and the Bogotá International Press in Colombia decided, in the same year, to publish an anthology to encourage more people to travel alone?

I think not.

Although in *Roam Alone* we do have a few stories by men, they are far outnumbered by those by women. I believe these two anthologies prove that women have made that final step to full equality with their male counterparts by travelling any route, by any means, and for any length of time they want. I love the comment by author Elizabeth O'Donnell in *Breaking in the Shoes of a Braver Woman*, the first essay you will read in *Alone Together*.

"I'll let you into a secret," she writes, "It's not that hard at all."

She's right. Travelling alone isn't that hard, once you've taken the initial plunge – but the anticipation often is. We need inspiring stories like these, stories from women who gave up good jobs, resisted the slide into self-doubt, and made a decision that would change their lives. They would travel, not in comfortable, reassuring Europe or the USA, but in Latin America, a region their friends and family warn them against. I'll let you into another secret too: the people of Latin America are the kindest, funniest, and most hospitable people you will meet anywhere in the world.

My first solo trip to the region was journeying through Central and South America to fulfil a long-held dream of seeing Machu Picchu, which in 1969 was not the tourist hot-spot of today. Indeed, when I did finally get there I was the only gringa amongst the dozen or so tourists. I made the mistake of agreeing to be accompanied through Mexico by a male American colleague. Disaster! It didn't take long to realise that two incompatible people with incompatible ideas of health and safety were never going to have the journey of a lifetime. Once I shed him at the Guatemalan border, my travels were transformed.

"At twenty-one or twenty-two I couldn't possibly have done this trip alone, but now that I'm old [I was twenty-eight!] you'd be amazed at how easy it is," I wrote to my sister. "Apart from occasional loneliness, which is inevitable, the only real problem is walking about cities alone at night, which is definitely unpleasant. But otherwise people fall over themselves to be nice. Drinks appear like magic whenever I'm thirsty, and at bus and train stations people always help with my luggage, find me a taxi, and usually pay the fare. And of course you get invited to people's homes." That is probably the trump card solo travellers have up their sleeves, especially women. People open their hearts and homes to lone travellers.

Travelling alone was, for me, life changing, but compiling the stories for *Roam Alone* and reading the tales in *Alone Together* was life affirming. Editors Karen Attman, Victoria Kellaway, and Emma Newbery had the same experience. Not all of the adventures we editors are sent can be included in our books, but of course we read them all, enjoy them all, admire the writers who have described their journeys, and store their experiences vicariously so we can relay them to any potential traveller who asks, "Really? On my own?"

– **Hilary Bradt MBE**, founder of Bradt Travel Guides
(www.bradtguides.com)

Prologue

When I announced I was off to travel solo around South America back in 2013, people were shocked. In fact, the reactions of my terrified colleagues were so shrill they could be heard reverberating down the stairwell, out into the street, and down into the London Underground where their words caught on like an echo… "You know you're gonna die, right? You know you're gonna die, right?"

Why is it that when a woman declares that she's about to embark on an exciting solo life adventure, so many people seem to collectively lose their minds? You might only be spending a weekend alone in a city you've already visited but the way some people react, you may as well have revealed you're off to attempt living at the bottom of the ocean.

To women who've travelled before, it's amusing. You can laugh off the over-the-top warnings and lists of ways in which you might imminently meet your maker. You've travelled before so you know it's life-changing magic. But to those who have yet to travel, these comments can be a little more insidious. If the people that know you and care about you think it's a bad idea, perhaps it is? Maybe you really shouldn't book that ticket.

We can't have that.

We women spend a good portion of our lives listening to ideas about what we should be doing. About how strong we are, what we can 'manage,' what we should have, and want, and need. It's pretty nuts really that still today, when women have spent centuries venturing into unchartered territory, curing disease, and circumnavigating the globe in boats, on bikes and on foot, that people still think they have the right to tell us the same thing they always have – that we'd be better off staying at home.

The tales you'll read in *Alone Together* are from women who've refused to listen to this. Women who've overcome their own fears and decided to listen to that inner voice – the one that says, 'Pack those bags mate, you've got a whole world to see.'

Travelling alone is a wonderful thing. If I close my eyes, put my hair dryer on its gentle setting and aim it at my face, it's almost like I'm there. Travelling. Learning about the world and myself. Taking the time to discover what makes me tick and what I'm made of. Meeting dozens of women doing exactly the same thing. Women refusing to be put off by nerves or by what other people think of them. This is what makes me smile the most about this book – the overwhelming desire these women have to see more, to do more, and to be more. This is a powerful glimpse at what you can learn about yourself when you take time away from 'normal life' and decide to pay attention.

Alone Together is a refreshingly realistic look at what happens when you travel solo. There are no fairy tales here. These are accounts of real women, exploring the real world. The writers share their giddy highs, their successes, the moments that taught them what they're made of or that set them on the right path. They bravely share their reasons for breaking free, the mistakes they made, the dangers they faced, and the places they ventured to that scared them. These women are bright, determined and fully aware of the risks – they just happen to know they're capable of handling them. You are too. *Alone Together* lets you in on a solo female traveller secret – it's perfectly normal to be nervous, stubborn and even a little suspicious… as long as you don't let it stop you from living.

We tend to read books because we seek knowledge, inspiration or empowerment. This book provides all three. It's for those who've travelled alone before and who can't wait to do it again. For those who are currently in the process. For those who've travelled with friends and can't help wondering what it might be like to set off alone. But most importantly, *Alone Together* provides knowledge, inspiration and empowerment for those of you teetering on the edge of taking the plunge. Peering towards the horizon. Wondering what might happen if you just packed it all in, laced up your shoes, and walked towards it.

What you're about to read will persuade you to do exactly that.

— **Amy Baker,** Author of *Miss-Adventures: A Tale of Ignoring Life Advice While Backpacking Around South America*

Breaking in the Shoes of a Braver Woman

Elizabeth O'Donnell

In the space of a year I was unjustly fired, my long-term boyfriend dumped me and moved out, my housemates followed and my subsequent self-destructive behaviour didn't inspire much loyalty in my remaining friends. I writhed in self-pity for far too long before I realised the freedom that came with losing everything: there was nothing holding me back.

I had settled for a safe, comfortable lifestyle and the rug had been ripped from under my feet. My self-confidence was shattered and the dream of backpacking Latin America felt like it belonged to someone much bolder and more capable than me. I told myself I should work on my mental health first and build up my confidence. I was waiting until I felt ready but delaying only made things worse.

It was on a day spent entirely in bed, too anxious to leave the house and too upset to contact anyone for help, that I realised I needed to do something drastic or that readiness might never come. If I already felt this terrible, this frightened, inside my wilted comfort zone, then what did I really have to lose?

I booked a flight to Mexico, bought a backpack, got five vaccinations and transferred the money I'd been half-heartedly saving for a house deposit onto a travel card, all whilst fighting the urge to vomit. I had never travelled alone before nor been to a developing country, and I didn't speak a word of Spanish.

Everyone I told immediately blurted out their most chilling horror story: gangs, guns, thieves, abductions, murder, rape, sex-trafficking, malaria and deadly parasites. My boss at the time actually grabbed me and prayed aloud to Jesus for my protection and the wisdom to make the right choices. I got so sick of people tearing up as they looked at me as if it would be the last time they'd ever see me, that I stopped telling people at all. I even deactivated my Facebook when an article popped up about a backpacker who died taking a selfie at Machu Picchu.

The flight itself was a living nightmare of squirming anxiety and terror: what have I done? This is the worst mistake of my entire life. I'm going to die alone in Mexico. I walked from the arrivals gate as if I were heading towards a firing squad, and stepped shakily into a taxi.

I flinched as I heard footsteps and shouts heading towards me, "*Tu libro, tu libro!*" It was the smiling immigration officer handing me the book I'd forgotten and left on her desk. For a moment I hoped she'd noticed my total incompetence and was here to drag me by the ear onto the first plane back to Australia. But she only waved with a cheerful "*Bienvenida!*" and slammed the door of the taxi, which closed like a casket.

The taxi sped out of the airport before I could buckle my seatbelt, and as I turned to look out the window I felt the weight of the world slip away. I was here. It was happening. Adrenaline flooded my heart and I felt a kind of ecstasy I had never felt before, but would come to know well over the next year.

Mexico City was a contrast of ramshackle structures against stylish town houses, tangles of trees, colourful bunting and striking street art. The balmy air drifted through the open window. It brought the scent of copal resin and Palo Santo incense, along with the aroma of sizzling street food. I saw a man walking a dozen dogs at once, school children stuffing *taquitos* into their mouths, and a rickshaw stacked high with coconuts threatening to tumble off. Vendors stood in traffic poking newspapers and bottles of water at drivers, or simply juggling swords and flames. My driver dropped a coin into the palm of one such street entertainer before fiddling with the scratchy radio. Inexplicably, Men At Work's "Down Under" blasted from the speakers and I was beside myself laughing.

In those first few weeks I sought out seasoned solo female travellers with wide-eyed wonder. They seemed to emit an aura of confidence, a self-assured glow without a shred of ego. More importantly, they held the informed and honest answers I was seeking. Only women who have been to the places you are headed can offer you advice on travelling there as a woman. This sounds obvious but it's important that you actively ignore the fear-mongering of others, especially those with outdated guidebooks. There was no sense of competition or hyperbole among these women. We were all on the same team and determined to help each other grow and feel safe.

Encouraged and emboldened by this new truth, I went on to achieve more than I could ever have dreamed. In Guatemala I hiked four thousand metres above sea level to the summit of Acatenango and cried tears of disbelief watching a neighbouring volcano erupt in the setting sun. I swam with turtles and whale sharks in Mexico and playful eagle ray fish in Belize. I scaled an underground waterfall with a slippery rope, the only light cast by the candlestick lodged between my teeth. I went night diving in Honduras under the cloak of the new moon and witnessed the stunning phenomenon of bioluminescence – it was as though I was swimming in a sky full of stars.

I slept in a hammock on the island of Ometepe in the center of Lake Nicaragua, listening to the roar of the jungle at night. I hopped through the San Blas Islands of Panama and crossed the border into Colombia, sliding out of the boat and wading over to the immigration office in a fit of laughter. I jumped into moving buses through the rear door, hitchhiked to breathtaking waterfalls in Costa Rica and rode on the back of a dirt bike up into the hills of Colombia's Sierra Nevada. I swung from ropes, leapt from cliffs, and dove through underground caves. I felt the two hands of fear and doubt snake their way around my ankles and yank me backwards over and over until eventually, I shook them for good.

As fun as it is to encourage the myth that what I did was wildly exotic and dangerous, I'll let you in on a secret: it's not that hard at all. I have been overwhelmed by the kindness of strangers, the mutual trust of travellers, and the generosity of the poor. Latin America is enjoying a flourishing tourism industry that's developing fast, and they have everything laid out ready for you. Locals knew where I was going before I did, and would point me in the right direction without my ever having to ask. Hostels organise social activities, cheap and cheerful communal meals, day trips, tours and onward transport in seconds – you don't even have to leave your hammock.

There are so many other solo travellers to team up with that unless you put in a conscientious effort, you won't end up getting much time to yourself. There are nifty new apps, free Wi-Fi nearly everywhere, and book exchanges overflowing with guidebooks that have handwritten tips in the margins – it's almost too easy. That's not to say you don't need to exercise caution, but no more so than you have your whole life as a woman in this world. Arm yourself with knowledge, be alert, be conscious but above all, do not fear.

It was bizarre when people started to compliment me on my courage, and other girls started to look at me the way I had looked at women I admired. My family boasted and told me how proud they were, which wasn't something I was used to. For a while it made me feel uncomfortable and confused – was I a fraud? I always thought confidence was something you're born with, or that it suddenly kicks in like puberty and that I was simply a late bloomer.

I've come to learn that confidence is something you have to discover within yourself. I didn't feel capable of doing any of the things I've done this year, but I surprised myself by doing them anyway. The nerve to have a go doesn't come from confidence exactly, it's something closer to recklessness, desperation, curiosity or desire. I'm talking about the moment of accomplishment, the intoxicating sensation of relief when you relief when you realise you were wrong about yourself. It's a renewed hope deep down that maybe you can do anything after all. From here, confidence spreads like a virus through your whole being, it's contagious, and anyone is capable of catching it.

My mother, a strong figure in my life, is an over-thinker like me, and I pushed her anxiety to the limits with this trip. Before I left, I tried to conceal my trepidation from her in a failed attempt to give her some peace of mind. Whether intentional or not, one thing she said gave me all I really needed.

She was driving me to an outdoor supplies store and I was cracking jokes about needing waterproof boots to kick piranhas away in the Amazon.

Looking sideways at me, her voice dropped to a serious tone. "Aren't you scared?"

I felt the knot in my stomach shift and force its way up my throat like a fist. My eyes welled up with tears, and I tried to swallow them, but the truth came out.

"Of course I am. I'm terrified."

She was thrown off by my sincerity but she clicked her tongue valiantly and retorted, "Oh for God's sake, if you don't like it you can just come back."

And with that one line she had set me free. It was okay if I failed! Once you accept this, things get a little easier. Love is fleeting, friendships deteriorate, objects break, jobs and houses can be lost, but nobody can take your experiences away from you. No relationship in your life is more important than the one you have with yourself. Don't live vicariously. If you've ever thought about doing something like this, do it.

And don't you dare let being a woman hold you back.

Elizabeth O'Donnell

Elizabeth is a twenty-six year-old writer from Perth, Western Australia. She enjoys a vegan lifestyle and is a passionate environmentalist and feminist. Her love of literature has given her a wild imagination and a voracious sense of adventure. Elizabeth travelled from Mexico through Central and South America in 2016 and is currently at home enjoying time with her family. She hopes to see more of Europe, Africa, and the Middle East in the next few years. This is the first time she has shared her writing with the world but, as Anaïs Nin wrote, "The day came when the risk to remain tight in a bud was more painful than the risk it took to blossom." Follow Elizabeth at www.instagram.com/eventuallyyyyy.

A Sticky Revelation

Teresa Bruce

On the page, I won't try to fake it. I'm nervous traveling to Honduras on a business trip as a woman alone. My mind keeps replaying a story I heard about criminals who stole the rings off a woman's finger as she walked her dog and then shot the dog just because.

In person, for the sake of professionalism, I muster all the buck-up pluck I imagine more fearless travelers display.

After all, I have been to this country before: as a seven-year-old stowaway in my father's hot, homemade camper. I loved traveling through Latin America then and when a power outage zaps the air-conditioning of San Pedro Sula's Intercontinental Hotel, it is just a sweaty slide back in time. I was too young to understand the turmoil stirring just under the surface of this and almost every Central American country in the 1970s. By the time my family reached Honduras, the sight of men with machine guns slouched under banana trees was as normal as the barefoot kids who brought us bread when we camped for the night.

So it feels natural, in a way, to have an armed driver deliver me from location to location in modern-day Honduras, dodging crater-sized potholes on the long drive up a mountain to Lake Yojoa. I will be bringing a crew here to film one of the country's first aquaculture operations: tilapia cordoned off from the rest of a fresh-water lake nestled in a depression formed by volcanoes. The farther away from the city we drive, the more I let go of my fears. The atmosphere is exotic and ethereal and catapults memories of Central America from the faded images of my childhood into a vivid immediacy.

My client ties up our canoe at an elaborate floating dock where I snap photographs of workers dumping sacks of pelleted fish food into the netted underwater enclosures. In a whirling instant, the surface is transformed from placid to frothing with hungry fish, and I realize that the money shot will be underwater. But from the surface of Lake Yojoa it is impossible to tell whether it will be feasible to shoot without underwater lights.

There is only one way to find out: taking a look for myself. Somewhere buried in my backpack is a disposable, waterproof camera – a low-tech backup just in case I need to take location pictures in a downpour. I'm wearing a bathing suit under my clothes and strip down to it while my client turns his back.

I'm about to take the plunge when one of the workers shouts out a warning. He points to the watch I've forgotten to take off my wrist. I gulp. It was the first present my husband Gary ever gave me and I'm about to ruin it. I'm shoving it into the change pocket of my jeans, wadded up on the dock, when I realize it's probably just as stupid to jump in with my wedding ring. It's the first time I've taken it off and I have never felt more naked as I do diving headfirst into thousands of slippery tilapia.

The bulging, glassy eyes of the fish seem to magnify underwater, especially when a woman with a camera plunges into their midst. I am kicking my way through walls of tilapia, my bare skin bumping against fluttering fins, gaping fish lips, and solid flanks of glittering scales. I raise the camera upwards, shooting into streams of sunlight.

Back at the surface I'm still gasping as my client hands me an empty burlap feed bag and points to my soaking wet hair.

"Oh that's okay," I tell him, too exhilarated even to shiver. "It'll just dry off on the boat ride back."

He bites his lip. "Um, actually it's not that. You just might want to clean off a bit. It'll be harder to get it out when it dries."

I run my ringless hand through my hair and discover that it is smothered in tilapia poop, clumps and strings of it clinging to every strand of hair. The burlap sack simply grinds it deeper into my scalp. I reach for my shirt and wipe my face. Yup, I'm coated in a fine layer of fish excrement. Time to get back to a hot shower as quickly as possible.

I'm in such a hurry that I yank my jeans up over still-wet, sticky thighs. I don't even hear the splash. In my peripheral vision I spot a swarm of tilapia following my shiny silver watch as it sinks to the depths of Lake Yojoa. I would bawl, but then the fish shit would stream into my mouth. My heart stops as I remember the second piece of jewelry I shoved into my jeans for safekeeping: my wedding ring.

I'm scared to poke my fingers where the watch once was. I feel the metal rivet of the change pocket first, too studded and small. This can't be happening. I should never have come here alone. I dig around, my fingers clumsy and numb from the cold water. But finally I feel it, the thinnest ridge of everything-is-going-to-be-okay poking into my hip. I hold it there, pressed against my flesh, until my breathing returns to normal. I slide it onto the ring finger of my shaking left hand and clasp my fist against ever losing it again.

Someday a chef is going to slice open a fillet of Honduran tilapia and discover an undigested Kenneth Cole watch. It may still tick, counting down the seconds and minutes of an overscheduled, stressed-out woman's life. I don't really have time for epiphanies but one seems to have caught up with me.

I have let the outside world color the trust that I normally have in my decisions and myself. I am rushing through what should be the best year of my life, cramming the hours of every day with ambition and obligation. But it is my watch at the bottom of Lake Yojoa and not my wedding ring. If that isn't a sign to slow down and reboot my priorities, then I don't know what is.

I call Gary the minute I get back to the hotel, hair still crusty with fish poop but too desperate to hear his voice to shower

first.

"You'll never guess what happened," he says, before I get a word in. "My dad saw a 1968 Avion camper in the Milwaukee classifieds. He says it's in pretty good shape and the guy only wants US$1,200 for it."

Without hesitation, I tell him to start looking for a truck big enough to handle it. After all, we'll need something dependable on the Pan-American Highway. Because as soon as this film is over we are going to find the camper of my childhood.

Teresa Bruce

Teresa is a communications strategist, screenwriter, and TEDx speaker. Her essay is adapted from her 2017 travel memoir *The Drive: Searching for Lost Memories on the Pan-American Highway*, which she also narrated for Audible. Her PBS documentary *God's Gonna Trouble the Water* won a CINE Golden Eagle, and her first memoir, *The Other Mother: a Rememoir*, won an Independent Book Publishers Association Benjamin Franklin Gold Medal. She lives between Washington DC, and Beaufort, South Carolina, USA, and blogs daily at www.teresabruce.me.

Home is a Loaded Word

Elizabeth Holli Wood

"Look," my grandfather says, removing the orange baseball cap I had bought him. He points to a seam that has already come loose at the back and made a hole near the strap.

"China," he laughs, in his harsh staccato way. My grandfather's laugh is ancient, I think. It's the way I imagine a Velociraptor's grandfather would have laughed.

"The woman I married, she went back," he snorts in his loud Cuban Spanish and his accent clips the 's' sounds away as if with a machete. At this point I realize he has remembered I am Elizabeth – he is wearing the hat in honor of my visit, after all – but he has forgotten for now that this means I'm his granddaughter. I suddenly feel ashamed that my living in New York City is starting to take its toll. Still, it's hard to feel too bad about refusing to orient my life around a ninety-four year-old man who, if I am honest, is being a little ungrateful about my gift.

My grandfather swore he would never return to Cuba and he actively encouraged his children to feel the same way. Every time the country was mentioned to my brothers, my cousins and I, it was in a way that suggested we couldn't visit Cuba because it was no longer a real place, it was a memory locked in the past. I feared that if I ever visited I would create a parallel reality that was out of step with our simultaneous existence in the United States.

But then international policy, in its infinite wisdom, made a whole country reappear. When the travel restrictions to Cuba were finally loosened, a missing piece reappeared on my mental map. I realized that what had been a forgotten country for many had felt like a forbidden country to me, and the reasons for that now seemed faraway. Within weeks, I had a ticket south. When I entered Fort Lauderdale airport holding my legal visa to a country that had been more legend than landmass for my entire life, I felt like I had discovered that Narnia was accessible, if you only knew a guy.

My grandfather's English is non-existent and my Spanish is a coward. We're sitting in his home in Florida and I'm attempting to share the pictures from my solo trip across Cuba, from Havana to Camagüey, and back. My vocabulary is labored and I rely on aggressive gestures towards the photos I have taken. I fast forward through the scenes shot from the window of a Cuban bus and the images of banana leaves and the palm trees framed by the sun. My grandfather refuses to focus on the photos I have taken of would-be passengers on the side of the road, waving cash in their outstretched hands as they clamor for a ride.

I'm surprised he doesn't recognize the houses and the buildings in Camagüey, because I know they were there when he left. He's not interested in the pictures of his family either, even though I'm desperate to prove to him that they took me in with open arms, that they put me up and fed me *tamales*. One of them, my great-aunt Lourdes, even greeted me with a great slap on my backside and declared that it was obvious we were family because our hips do not lie.

The excitement I feel over my stories is lost on him. Even my mother looks visibly bored with her role as translator, filling in the gaps whenever my Spanglish gets too much. I want to say to them both, "I'm so sorry I'm boring you with pictures of your homeland," but I doubt my sarcasm will translate and I know my lousy vocabulary is probably a blessing. 'Homeland' is a loaded term for someone who has spent more than fifty years on the right or wrong side of a revolution, depending who you ask.

The next photo I show is the one I took of my great-aunt and her daughter in the peach-tiled home they share. The doors and windows are open so the light December crosswind can break up the heat. It's not clear in the picture, but I remember that the blue, synthetic lace curtains were dancing in the breeze. My mother scoffs as she spots my cousin sitting on a vinyl lawn chair in the living room, her sandaled toe brushed against the dusty floor.

"She's a doctor. They're all doctors there," she says. "Can you imagine being a doctor and living like that?" I choose not to highlight the irony of expecting our doctors in the U.S. to demand shining and pristine floors at all times, and the fact most of those floors are cleaned by women who look like Cuban doctors.

Going to Cuba was not the first time I had defied my grandfather, but it was definitely the best. It was the first time I experienced how it felt to be in a world where families that look like my own are the norm. Before Cuba, I'd never stayed in a *casa particular* either, hosted by strangers who kissed my cheeks in homes filled with children who would have given me the lollipops out of their mouths if I had wanted them. I'd never seen students in school uniforms sing songs about chickens that cry "*Pio! Pio! Pio!*" when they're hungry.

Now I'm hiding the Che Guevara hats I purchased for my friends at the bottom of my duffel bag and attempting to explain to my grandfather why it had been so important for me to go and see this world for myself, by myself, but with family – including him – on my mind at every step. It's unfortunate that the only way I can tell him this is with my mangled Spanish. After the odd misstep, he indignantly confirms that he had never been with me, not at all, that I was mistaken and he would never go back. I've clearly agitated him and it's even harder to keep up with what he is shouting. My mom tells me he is yelling about a program on television he wants to see in his room, but if we go out for food later we should bring him something back.

I stop my grandfather before he disappears into the world of scantily clad *señoritas* bouncing around on his television screen. I want to tell him about the people I met when I traveled in his first country. I want him to be grateful that they kept me safe.

I hope he might want to know that it was my driver, Ángel, who negotiated my bus ticket to Camagüey by bribing the lady at the ticket counter for me. I want him to laugh at the thought that Ángel and I sat together in the parking lot, chain-smoking cigarettes and eating Twizzlers, until five o'clock in the morning when the bus finally arrived.

I hope my grandfather might want to hear about César, the man I met on the bus who put his hands on my shoulders and warned me that the current U.S. president reminds him too much of the leaders in Cuba's past, and that we all know "how that turned out." Perhaps he would be impressed that César and I exchanged email addresses and that we plan to write to one another. Perhaps he would think me a woman of the world.

Maybe he would want to know that my cousin Daisy, that "tall drink of water" as Cubans like to call her, a woman who proves Cubans can be born with long legs too, took me dancing and made me a tasty flan. Maybe he would be amused that my second cousin's new wife, Tonia, took me from office to office to visit my family as they worked, and not once did any of their bosses throw us a sharp look or clear their throat conspicuously to force them back to work.

Maybe he would also like to know that while, yes, his great-grandnephew Oreidis is a devoted patriot, he is also a talented journalist who draws comics, speaks three languages, and cares for his elderly family members in the home where my grandmother grew up. That's the same home from which my grandfather plucked my grandmother to marry her – three children, six-plus decades and a country-shaped life change ago.

Instead, I tell my grandfather about the police officer who gave Ángel such a stern look he turned his thumping music down to a whisper. I tell him about the civilian on the bicycle who questioned me, aggressively, as to whether I had been drinking during Fidel Castro's official mourning period. I know I am pandering to his conceptions of modern Cuba, but it works. He and my mom share a knowing laugh, and that means I'm allowed his company for a few minutes more.

My grandfather slips into another high-decibel story about the time he witnessed the burning of the sugar crops. Most of it goes over my head and my mom has heard it a thousand times. She shrugs and asks what I would like for dinner.

I manage to show my grandfather one last picture from my final day in Havana, a photograph I had taken after a thundering downpour. In the photo, an orange cat grips a gray kitten by its gruff. Against the backdrop of chain link fences and pastel walls smothered in graffiti, I had watched and followed the mother cat as she dragged her kitten five exhausting blocks.

Both cats stare ahead in my photo, neither appears to question their situation as they move from one dusty clay gutter to the next. My grandfather looks at the cats, laughs his eternal laugh, and leaves.

Elizabeth Holli Wood

Elizabeth is a writer and creator of the podcast *The Future is Gross*. She explores how access to technology and the ethics of product innovation shape culture in unlikely and sometimes creepy ways. She believes in the power of people, not profits, to advance society and make lives better. Elizabeth currently lives in New York City, USA, but has aspirations to live on every continent. As the proud daughter of a Cuban-born mother and a father with British-Honduran heritage, she looks forward to many more visits to Latin America, alone or otherwise. Tweet Elizabeth at @elizabethholli.

At the Mercy of Men

Sissi Korhonen

I started my journey across Latin America in Ushuaia, Argentina, and I have been solo cycling slowly, yet steadily, through heaven and hell ever since. In the past two years I've crossed the isolated valleys of Patagonia, the palm-dotted coastal villages of Uruguay, the Alpine-like communities of Southern Brazil, the infamous drug-trafficking regions of Colombia and Paraguay, the harsh Bolivian highlands, the cold Peruvian mountains and the humid Ecuadorian rainforests.

Although I've had a good look at this continent's biodiversity, I've been most struck by the diversity of its peoples, the influence of Europe mixed with ancient indigenous traditions, the connection between nature and modernity, old and new, rich and poor, men and women. These are contrasts that continue to take me by surprise.

Nothing has left me more in awe than the hospitality shown by Latin Americans. "*Mi casa es tu casa*" (my home is your home) is not an urban legend or a cliché that lacks significance for local people. It's reality. A guest is treated like a member of the family, if not better. A thirsty long-distance cyclist is offered beverages and a hungry traveler is offered food, most often by the non-wealthy who are used to sharing what little they own.

I haven't had many desperate moments but there was one day, right at the beginning of my trip, when I really felt like going home. I was cycling across the Argentinian pampa after two months of lovely experiences. What does a Finn do at a time like that? A Finn thinks, "Wow! Things are going just a little too well. When is something sketchy going to happen?" Two minutes later I realized a small bag with my ID, my credit card, and some money had fallen off at a crossing where I had stopped for a toilet break, some fifty kilometers earlier.

There was a farm nearby, so I asked the owners if I could leave my bicycle with them while I hitchhiked back to the crossing. "Of course," they said. I went back, found my bag and thought, "Wow! What amazing luck," and I started cycling again.

Thirty kilometers later, a truck passed by very close to me. I moved out of the way and fell into a ditch. I was bleeding when I emerged, there were scratches on my knees and elbows and the handlebars of my bike looked a bit weird. No biggie. I cleaned myself up, fixed my bike and thought, "Wow! That could've been so much worse."

I cycled another thirty kilometers. My destination of the day now lay just ten kilometers away. Hungry and tired, having pedaled for one hundred and thirty-five kilometers, I began to crave salted peanuts. Dreaming of them, I cycled a little further and then I saw a sealed bag of caramelized nuts on the side of the road. Would you think that was a gift from above and stop? I did. I picked up the bag and continued…well, I tried to continue. My gears wouldn't switch. I tried again. Nothing. Too tired to think, I tried again (what idiot does that?) and then I watched as my entire rear derailleur twitched and fell off.

There were plenty of cars passing so I decided to try to hitchhike with my bicycle to the next town. No-one picked me up. I was totally ignored. Suddenly, a pickup truck pulled over and three heavily tattooed men got out and began to walk towards me (Cool. My mother's worst nightmare). The men decided to help me with the power of thought and watched as I tried to convert my bicycle into a single-speed. I'd never done that before, nor had I seen it done. But I'd heard it was possible so I measured the chain, cut it and used my chain link to put everything back into place. Or that's what I thought. I got back on my bike with a feeling of immense pride and watched as the men drove away.

I stamped my pedal once and the chains jammed completely.

What did I think this time? "Oh, shit."

I had no choice but to try to hitch-bike again. I stuck my thumb out by the side of the road and caught the attention of two Harley-Davidson guys on their motorcycles (my mother's nightmare continues). They asked if my bicycle, its four panniers, and I wanted to get on one of their bikes. Not really. That didn't seem too safe to me. We thought about it and came up with a better solution that involved one of their motorbikes, my bicycle and a rope. Yes, I was towed ten kilometers by a Harley-Davidson

I arrived at the next town only to be told I wouldn't be able to fix my bicycle unless I made it to the next big city, which was forty kilometers away. I still couldn't ride the bike and much as I was grateful to the Harley-Davidson gentlemen, I didn't feel like hanging onto a rope for a further forty kilometers. I began to ask the drivers at a petrol station whether there was anyone who could take me to Bahía Blanca but all of the cars were full. That is, until a truck driver walked up and offered to take me (Mom, please wake up now). I tied my bicycle to the back of his truck and climbed inside. He was a great guy and offered me coffee and *mate* (Argentinian herbal tea). I was in heaven.

We reached the city in less than an hour. Night fell and my broken bike and I found ourselves somewhere in the suburbs where there were no street lights, trying to find the house of a Couchsurfing host who hadn't responded since his first message a week ago. Nor was he expecting me to arrive so soon. I navigated to his address with just three percent of battery life left on my phone. Luckily, my host was home.

He opened the door, invited me inside and offered me a homemade dinner, a warm shower and a soft bed. And, perhaps needless to say, he had no further intentions. In fact, he had only one thing on his mind.

"*Mi casa es tu casa*," he said.

Sissi Korhonen

Sissi is a freelance journalist, blogger, and communications consultant from Finland. She has dedicated her life to exploring, interpreting, and creating content on female empowerment, intercultural phenomena, intriguing people, and alternative lifestyles. She has lived in eight countries, speaks seven languages, and has traveled the Americas, Africa and Europe, mostly by hitchhiking and long-distance cycling. Sissi has also worked as a camerawoman, scriptwriter, and HR consultant. She holds a BA in Social and Cultural Studies and an MA in Intercultural Communication and is the co-founder and owner of *Seikkailijattaret*, a Finnish online travel media for women. Visit Sissi's blog at www.strangerless.com and follow her on Twitter and Instagram: @strangerless.

Journalist: Don't Shoot

Ronnie Lovler

My connection with Latin America is a feeling, as if the region reached out and touched me from afar. We connected, or at any rate I connected, from the very first moment at my very first stop.

I worked for CBS and CNN in Latin America between 1984 and 1996, when there was heightened interest in local developments: the Contra War in Nicaragua, the civil war in El Salvador, the U.S. invasion of Panama, the early years of Hugo Chavez in Venezuela, Chile without Pinochet (or at least without Pinochet in a leadership role), and Peru under Alberto Fujimori. I lived in Nicaragua, El Salvador, Panama, Chile, and Colombia. Before that, I lived in Puerto Rico for seven years. Six of them were with *The San Juan Star*.

My first trip to Central America was in 1982, where I was part of a small team from Pacifica Radio covering the El Salvador elections. Was I frightened? Of course. This was a country where death squads were active and had murdered hundreds, if not thousands, of their own people, where four Catholic missionaries from the U.S. had been killed, and Archbishop Óscar Romero was assassinated while offering Mass. I was in over my head but I didn't realize that until we covered the voting at the polls in downtown San Salvador.

We hired a taxi and shared it with a videographer from Chile. That happened all the time, journalists pairing up with other journalists. We attached a white flag to our antenna to indicate that we were press. The gunshots started when we arrived at the polling station and found ourselves caught in the crossfire between guerrilla fighters and the Salvadoran military.

I hit the floor of the taxi, protecting my tape recorder because I didn't know what else to do. I didn't look up and I didn't look out and it didn't occur to me to record what I was hearing. I was new to the game and thinking only about not being shot. Before I had fully processed what was happening, it was over. My two U.S. colleagues and I were fine. The Chilean videographer, who had stepped out to film, was not. We found some volunteers from El Salvador's Green Cross and they took him to a hospital, but he died. A few years later I attended a photo exhibit of his work in Chile, held in his memory.

In 1988 I began reporting for CNN from El Salvador and I later experienced a similar incident when my videographer, Hugo Burgos, was shot. He was hit, probably by a rebel combatant, while filming from a military helicopter as it flew over a conflict zone. Hugo survived but he never recovered full use of his arm.

While at the hospital with Hugo and his mother in El Salvador, before CNN medevaced him to Miami, all I could remember was our dinner the previous night at the Camino Real hotel, where most of the international journalists were staying. The city had been on lockdown because of a guerrilla offensive and the military wouldn't let anyone out after dark. Hugo and I had shared wine and conversation and I had felt incredibly close to him.

The following morning the hundreds of journalists staying at the hotel awoke to the news that six Jesuit priests and two others had been murdered the previous night at their residence on the Central American University campus. We later learned that members of the Salvadoran military had carried out the killings.

Most journalists knew the Jesuits. They were outspoken critics of the war and advocates for the negotiation of a settlement between the government and the Faribundo Marti National Liberation Front. The Jesuits were always available to talk to the press and provide sound bites or quotes to help put the civil war in perspective.

It was early when we heard the news. We left our breakfasts uneaten as we raced back to our rooms, grabbed our gear and headed out to continue our coverage. Hugo secured his fateful spot on that military helicopter.

We were neither unfeeling nor uncaring, but we had learned to live with a certain gallows humor by then. The Salvadoran Press Club had issued a t-shirt four years earlier that said "*Periodista: no dispare*" (Journalist: don't shoot). We wore them, but it didn't always help.

I traveled to Nicaragua for the first time in 1982. It was the early years of the Sandinistas and I wanted to see what life was like there, three years into the Sandinista revolution. I arrived at a small hotel in Managua behind Antojitos, one of the city's most popular restaurants. There were no seats inside but there were plenty of wrought iron tables outside, arranged around a tree with one of the widest trunks I have ever seen.

Antojitos became a favorite spot for me, particularly during the early Sandinista years. When you asked a server for an item on the menu they tended to respond, "*No hay*," (We don't have it). It was almost always "*No hay*" because of the informal but very effective U.S. economic blockade of the Sandinista government. Antojitos was a pleasant place to be, even if you couldn't order anything you really wanted to eat from the menu.

On my first night in Managua, I walked the streets and was struck by the number of kids I saw carrying guns. I say kids, because most of them were teenagers. Many had Soviet-made AK-47s because they were either part of the Sandinista Police Force or in the Sandinista Popular Army. They were so young and so friendly and, at that point, so devoted to their revolution. I stood out as a non-Nicaraguan and almost every person wanted to talk to me, to find out what I thought of their country and why I had come. I had never felt safer walking in a city after dark.

If you had been a teenager in Managua during those early, heady years, you would probably have identified with the Sandinistas too. Joining them would have been the thing to do in your neighborhood. You would have been old enough to remember 1978, 1979, and the victorious Sandinista march into Managua after dictator Anastasio Somoza fled. Joining the Sandinistas would have offered you a job – a poorly paid one, but a job nonetheless.

Life was already different in the countryside, where the contras were active. The contras, or counter-revolutionaries, were the right-wing militias who opposed the Sandinistas and were funded and supported by the U.S.

My first time in Nicaragua, I stayed for about a week. It was Easter season and I went to a Sandinista rally held to convince people that it was acceptable to work during *Semana Santa* (Holy Week). That's a traditional vacation time in Latin America and while no one would be expected to work Holy Thursday or Good Friday, the Sandinistas were trying to build up revolutionary fervor about working Tuesday and Wednesday. I don't think they were too successful. But I do recall that their rally was a party. There was music and vendors selling flavored ice stuffed into paper triangles. There were people waving Sandinista flags. I had never seen anything like it.

I met Larry at the rally, a U.S. journalist who was freelancing in Nicaragua. I can't remember how we connected, whether someone had given me his name or whether we met randomly. I thought it was cool that he was a freelance journalist and an idea began to take root in my mind.

Larry invited me to go to Pantasma, a rural community in northern Nicaragua, in the mountains of Jinotega. He was going to cover a recent raid there by a band of contras. There was only room for traffic to travel in one direction at a time and the roads were rocky and filled with potholes. The journey was like flying on a plane that had encountered turbulence for three hours straight.

I had never been in a place like Pantasma. The main street, if you can call it that, was a continuation of the dirt highway. It was a farming village surrounded by coffee and tobacco fields and, higher up the mountain, verdant rainforests. The contra attacks were only just beginning, but it was all people could talk about. They were afraid of going out to farm their lands, to pick coffee, to hail a jitney or climb on the back of a pickup truck when they needed to leave the village. We spent the night on rickety beds in the home of a woman who rented out rooms. We had a breakfast of *gallo pinto*, Nicaragua's rice and beans staple, tortillas and warm Coca-Cola. Electricity was hit or miss and the old refrigerator in the woman's house was more a place to store drinks than to keep them cold. I was cautioned not to drink the water, but to stick with warm Coke.

I returned to Pantasma two years later, to report on the aftermath of a contra attack that had killed forty-seven villagers. The contras had set fire to local agricultural cooperatives, the coffee storage office, the territorial and police militia posts and other property. Pantasma ended up being one of the villages hardest hit by the contra war.

When you live somewhere, even when you cover a war, it's not all blood and violence. There are fun things to report, too, which convey what makes a place unique. One such thing in Managua was the skill required to get around. Houses had no numbers and streets had no names. Addresses were based on reference points and, sometimes, the reference point was based on where something used to be, before the 1972 earthquake that destroyed Managua. That meant an address might be, for example, "Where the Pepsi Cola plant used to be," or "Where the big tree used to be," or, "Where the big dog used to live."

Where did I live? From La Terraza (a restaurant) three blocks south, one hundred feet west. Or, after going three blocks south, to the house with the big mango tree in the front yard. That quirky tale got more airtime on *CNN International* than many of my news reports about war and politics over the years. I think it aired twenty-one times. But it was a great story and it told you something about life in Nicaragua beyond politics and warfare.

While in Nicaragua, I married a Nicaraguan photographer and had two children. After my sons were born, I would travel to the United States and bring back disposable diapers in bulk, just to give you an idea of my priorities. I dealt with the humdrum everywhere – grocery shopping, getting the kids to school, obtaining visas or residency permits and doing my job, which was always far from routine. My husband and I eventually split up, when it was professionally time for me to leave Nicaragua and he chose to stay.

Why did I fall in love with Latin America? The blame lies with Puerto Rico, which was my first stop. I arrived as a volunteer and university graduate, a young woman in her early twenties who could not speak a word of Spanish. I had no car and no address. There were no cell phones then and no landline where I lodged. I thought it was an adventure, but my sister tells me I drove my middle-class Jewish parents fraught with worry.

I soon made friends and someone, a very nice someone called José, took me under his wing. He gave me a place to stay but, more than that, he showed me Puerto Rico, and I fell in love. Not so much with José, but with Puerto Rico.

My first challenge was learning Spanish. I was determined to speak it. José spoke English but most of his friends and the other people I met did not. I spent a lot of time being silent, listening to the babble of people speaking Spanish around me. I picked out a word here and there and, eventually, I dared to speak a few rudimentary phrases.

A few months later, I got a job with *The San Juan Star*, Puerto Rico's Pulitzer Prize winning English-language newspaper. I was hired as a proofreader and then I worked on the copy desk. We worked on typewriters and pages were laid out on Manila paper before the type was set in the back shop, or printing room. There was something exciting about seeing the newspapers roll off the press. I worked late shifts and would hang around after I was finished, just so I could see that happen.

After two years on the copy desk I became a feature writer for what was known as "the women's pages," then a "real" reporter covering politics and the environment. I loved my life. I was politically progressive in a place where it was okay to be that way. I met numerous Puerto Rican *independentistas* and got a reputation for being sympathetic to their cause. I learned to play dominoes when we had a two-week strike at the Star. I learned enough about dancing salsa to keep the beat and survive without embarrassing my partner. And I learned to speak Spanish.

Thirty years later, whenever I return to Puerto Rico, I'm still introduced as Ronnie Lovler, the reporter from *The San Juan Star*, even though the Star as we knew it no longer exists. I was able to pay one final visit to a favorite colleague shortly before he died and he signed for me the memoir he wrote about his life at the Star. I've tried to read it but it makes me too nostalgic and I've never managed to finish it.

Why did I leave Puerto Rico? I'm still not sure and sometimes I think I made a mistake. But we can't undo the past. I left because, at that time, I felt there was more I wanted to do. A few years later I got on a plane to El Salvador to begin my life as an international correspondent.

I lived in Chile for three years and it is still one of my favorite countries. On a clear day, I could see the Andes from my front porch in Santiago. When it was overcast, when the pollution was too bad, the mountains disappeared like magic.

At that time Chile was no longer a big international news producer. Democracy had come to the country, Pinochet was out, and Eduardo Frei was president. I often visited Argentina and Peru. Once, when covering a minor border conflict between Peru and Ecuador, a dozen other journalists and I jumped out of a small plane because the pilot refused to touch down. I'm not that brave, but I was that stupid. Everyone else jumped, I was the last one out. I was driven by the thought that

I wouldn't know what was happening and that I'd have to wait at an Ecuadorian military base for several days until my colleagues returned. It ended up being a good story, but I probably wouldn't do that again.

Today's journalists will likely never have the thrill we had of trying to beat the technological odds of getting our stories out. I dictated my newspaper stories over the phone. It could take up to an hour to connect through an operator and for the connection to be good enough for the person at the other end to understand me. Radio stories were transmitted through alligator clips that I attached to the phone after I uncoupled the receiver. We eventually had the ubiquitous Tandy 200, which I consider to be the first laptop, although we could only see eight lines of copy at a time.

There was nothing like the pressure of trying to make the window that had been purchased for our television stories either. We dashed to the government-owned communication center, almost always up several flights of stairs and watched as a technician slammed our tapes into the player. We held our breaths while the countdown tape rolled and watched as the story fed, first both tracks and then the sound feed that allowed the network to run parts of our stories as teasers. And then we had the sweet sense of relief that came when we knew our story had been received and our piece would air.

I lived in Colombia for two years and my last visit to the country was in June 2017, on my way home from a work trip to Brazil. I couldn't get that close without a quick peek again.

It was not a roughing-it trip. I stayed in a nice hotel near the airport and didn't even have to navigate public transport, because a friend came to collect me in her car. I live in sea level Florida and adjusting to Bogota's altitude was a challenge. The rain never ceased, but I did wander around two historic neighborhoods, Usaquén with its Sunday flea market, and the original Bogota in La Candelaria, where I meandered in and out of the museums.

Those three days were a homecoming. I mention them now

not because they were one of my most exciting experiences, but because they were necessary. Once you have lived in a country, it never leaves you. That's how I feel about all of my Latin American countries. They are a part of me, and always will be.

Ronnie Lovler

Ronnie was a correspondent and bureau chief for CNN in Nicaragua and Chile from 1987 to 1996. She arrived in Nicaragua as a freelancer in 1984 and has reported from every country in Latin America. She was a Knight International Journalism Fellow in Colombia from 2011-2012 and received a Transparency International grant in Colombia in 2013. Ronnie teaches journalism at the University of Florida in Gainesville, USA, where she lives. She writes for *Americas Duty Free & Travel Retail* magazine, covering the industry and profiling countries, and is a book editor. In her spare time (ha!) Ronnie likes to go hiking, visit museums, watch films, listen to live music, do a bit of salsa dancing, and of course, travel.

Havana Rewind

Courtenay Strickland

The cold water hits my body –
I was too hot from dancing to wait for it to warm up –
And suddenly it is nine years ago, in the year 2000.
I am in Havana again and the scent of twice-used cooking oil
permeates the air.
Malanga fries softly on the stove.
There is a faint rustling of plastic grocery bags being rinsed
and hung to dry.
I lie on the narrow bed of my little room with you, wrapped
in your arms.

Suddenly, piano music – unexpected – wafts through the
vents of the room's thin door.
So perfect that at first we thought it recorded, so brilliant
it took us whole minutes to understand that it came from the
dusty grand
long neglected in the decaying living room.

A reluctant artist plays – we did not even know he could –
and we are his hidden audience.
It is extraordinary, it is beautiful, it is so much more than we
expected,
so much more than we could have imagined.

And so we wait – silent, listening, holding our breath, hoping to make it last.

A small stretch of ocean away, Florida spins in chaos, but I don't care –

nothing could be farther.

Surrounded by the stifling, horrid beauty of this place

bajo el azul de tu misterio

Life kisses me and I kiss back.

And right now, in this time, it is enough.

And we hold each other –

Knowing already, in places deep

That it will not last.

Courtenay Strickland

Courtenay's passion for Latin America – somewhat unlikely given her upbringing as the daughter of a Baptist minister in small-town Georgia, USA – blossomed in teacher Kay Lowe's high school Spanish class. In 1995, Courtenay made her first trip to Cuba to research her undergraduate thesis and has since traveled to Mexico, Costa Rica, Panama, Argentina, Peru and Puerto Rico. In 2012, Courtenay moved with her infant son and then-husband to Colombia, where she launched her blog, *Barranquilla or Bust! International relocation and other leaps of faith*, and developed a consulting business grounded in her years of civil rights work for U.S. nonprofits. Courtenay holds a Bachelor of Arts in Latin American Studies from Yale University and lives in Medellin, Colombia. She has run four marathons on three continents and enjoys dancing casino rueda-style salsa. She can be found online at www.courtenaystrickland.com.

"Bajo el azul de tu misterio" is an album title from the band Jaguares.

It Has to be Now

Nuria Elkout

Where are you from? Where are you going? How long have you been travelling? Why Central America?

"If I hear one of those questions again, I'm going to vomit," I said to my friend as we packed our bags for our trip from Antigua to Lake Atitlán. Despite her initial apprehension, I convinced her to forego a shuttle bus and travel via chicken bus.

Of course, her trepidation was warranted. When we made the decision to travel in Guatemala, we were met with surprise, shock and warnings about our safety from our friends and family. Imagine their reaction if they had known we would travel via the nation's most interesting mode of transportation.

While chicken buses aren't known for their safety, it was daytime and I had already made this trip once before with another friend. I reassured her we'd be safe as we shuffled onto a converted school bus from the 1980s that was lavishly painted blue, red, and green. Along both sides of the bus and plastered throughout the interior was the name, Esmeralda. We laughed and smiled at one another as we boarded, giddy with excitement. We were happy to soak up the chaos, which was a refreshing change from the orderly bus stations back home and the luxury shuttle companies that litter Central America.

As we took our seats on the soon-to-be crowded bus, I breathed in the cold humid air that smelled of spices, wood chips, and exhaust. Looking out the window, I saw lush green forest and patches of fog.

A local woman joined us and suddenly we were three to a bench that was originally designed for two children. I couldn't help but feel that I understood, at last, where the name 'chicken bus' comes from. It all made sense, we were the chickens and we were stuffed into the bus in much the same way the poor animals are stuffed into their cages.

The original (and thankfully, Justin Bieber-less) "Despacito" blasted through the sophisticated surround-sound system not generally found on most motor vehicles. We sang along and danced in our seats to the song we knew all too well. We would have known the words even if we hadn't wanted to, since the song had been playing in most bars, restaurants, grocery stores, and, well, buses since we arrived in Central America. Women passengers dressed in traditional Mayan attire smiled at us, and some chose to dance along too. Our dance moves were magnified by the wide and frequent turns the bus made along the winding road that would lead us to Lake Atitlán.

Little did we know that our dance moves wouldn't be the only thing amplified by the dramatic turns of the bus. Amidst the scurrying of people hopping onto the bus and those who quickly scuttled off, the woman sitting beside us departed and we were able to relax our bodies, which we hadn't noticed we were holding so rigidly.

My friend then turned to me with a look of fear and desperation.

"I have to pee," she said.

We were about an hour away from our final destination. We had already paid our fare. There wouldn't be any stops remotely close to civilisation until we arrived. While we were adventurous, we weren't get-off-the-bus-in-the-middle-of-nowhere-to-pee-in-the-Guatemalan-woods adventurous. I pleaded with her to hold it a little longer.

"I can't. I have to go. It has to be now," she said.

She held her empty, disposable, one-litre water bottle in her hand and I knew what had to be done. I jumped to my feet, handed her a knife and she cut off the top of the bottle. Resignedly, she started pulling her pants down.

"WAIT!" I yelled. "There's a big turn coming up. I'll give you the signal."

My friend waited, giggling, as two army officials entered the bus.

"Don't stop near our seat, don't stop near our seat," she repeated under her breath as they moved by us and stopped about two rows behind us. We let out a sigh of relief.

"They can't see you," I said. "The road looks straight, now's your chance. Go!"

I turned the other way so I could block her from view. I couldn't see what was happening but I did hear a constant stream above her giggles. I was surprised when a few minutes had passed and she was still going; she wasn't kidding around. She finished and pulled up her pants. We looked at one another and burst out laughing.

Out of the corner of my eye I saw a woman dressed in traditional Mayan clothing. Her arms were crossed and she sat alone in her row. As our eyes met, her face changed from disgruntled to expressionless and then to a wry smile. She let out a single chuckle that shook her whole body backwards and then suddenly she returned to normal. We sat back to enjoy the rest of our journey with smiles on our faces.

Before our trip, the questions we received from family and friends were about safety. Little did we know we would have been better equipped if we had paid more attention to our bladders. Of course, we can't help but think how much easier our ordeal would have been if we were men.

Nuria Elkout

Nuria is proud to be a #NastyWoman. She grew up in Canada, where she spent the majority of her time between Toronto and Ottawa. The last four years she has been living, working, and travelling throughout Latin America and currently lives in Lima, Peru, where she works as a gender advisor, human rights activist, and life coach. Nuria encourages all women to travel the region without fear and explore its rich culture and nature.

Missing

Rebecca Hoffmann

The annoying little bling sound that Facebook generates when you receive a chat message clanged through the otherwise quiet room. Annoyed, both with myself for not turning the sound off on the computer, and with the person writing to me, I checked the message.

"I missed my flight," it said. Oh, God. Really? Earlier that day, I had sent a friend of mine in a cab to the airport. I had debated whether or not to go with her and had decided upon the more economical solution of letting her go alone. After all, I assumed she was an experienced solo traveler or, at least, an experienced traveler. But now this message.

In the taxi, I looked at the greyish suburbs of Buenos Aires as they passed our windows. Spring was slowly coming, but most days the weather was cold and grey. The male friend who had volunteered to accompany me to the airport chatted with the taxi driver, but I wasn't in chatty mode. My friend at the airport had stopped answering my messages. I looked at the buildings as we passed. What had happened to her? Surely, she had just run out of battery and would sit and wait for us in a café.

She was nowhere to be seen in the airport. The information desk told us to contact the police in case they had seen her. They hadn't, but they were immediately on the alert. Even though kidnappings are now uncommon in Buenos Aires, they do still happen. The officers said they would help us search the airport and then they would decide which steps to take.

Bling. It was that Facebook sound again. Before I could check the message, my phone started to vibrate in my hand. It was my friend. She was clearly upset. I used all the force I had inside me to try to calm her down while my heart was pumping at full speed. I was anxious about what might have happened. After all, this is Latin America. Even though I have never had any trouble myself, I've heard so many stories. Kidnapping. Rape. Disappearances. Stay focused, I ordered myself.

I asked my friend where she was, numerous times. She didn't know. In a hotel near the airport, she said. I asked for the address, and told her we would be there right away. She said she didn't know the address, and she started crying about her lost flight. I ordered her to go down to the reception and ask for the address and a direct number to the hotel – and for God's sake, to stay online. We hung up and I saw the message she had written: Ciudad Evita. About twenty kilometers from the airport. She could not have walked there alone. What had happened?

A few minutes later my phone vibrated again, and her Facebook picture appeared on the screen. A male voice spoke in Spanish. The voice claimed to be with my friend, and insisted she was fine. When my Argentinian friend, who had accompanied me to the airport, heard me speaking in Spanish, he waved at me to give him the phone. I did. His voice became sharp as he presented himself with his full name, and repeatedly asked the voice on the other end to do the same. Hanging up, he turned to me and said: "It's a taxi driver. He will bring her back to the airport in twenty minutes. We must contact the police."

Boom, boom, boom. The sound of boots against the floor. Running. I looked around and saw at least ten uniformed police officers heading towards the airport's various exits. We walked quickly beside two more uniformed officers. One, a small woman in her mid-thirties, spoke to me. Time was running out, she said. We had to be at the place where the supposed taxi driver had told us to be. We jumped in the back of her police car.

It all felt so surreal. Almost like a bad action movie. But it was real life, and I was in the middle of it. I always say when I watch action movies that I could never be a police officer. My nerves are simply not made for it. Now I had no choice but to pull myself together, and get my friend out of whatever situation she had found herself in.

The police car dropped us off and we stood freezing in the late afternoon on a road leading to the airport. A car arrived. We had agreed with the police that as soon as we got my friend out of the car, they would approach the driver. My friend seemed perplexed when we approached. I told her to get out of the car, and asked if she had everything with her. Passport? Money? Mobile? She was confused, and did not understand the situation nor why I was so calm.

When she saw five uniformed police officers approaching, she panicked. She started to shout and ask what was going on. The police asked if the taxi driver had harmed her. At first, she repeated over and over again that he was a nice guy, and she did not want to answer their questions about what had happened. Fractions of truth were slowly revealed. Yes, he had tried to touch her. Yes, he had tried to take off her clothes. Yes, she had said no. Still, he had continued.

We spent the rest of that night at the police station.

Little by little, bits and pieces came together. When my friend had arrived at the airport, the staff at the check-in counter had told her that she had exceeded the possible check-in time for her flight. Unable to cope with that, she had gone outside for a cigarette to calm her nerves and had been approached by a man some ten years older than herself. He had asked her for a cigarette, and had asked her what was wrong. After chatting for some time, he had offered to drive her to a hotel where she could stay for the night. Blindly trusting the good in people, and the authority of an official airport taxi driver, she had agreed. In the car, he had offered her beer from a used plastic bottle, which she had accepted. The police officers just looked at each other when she said that, but they decided not to do a drug test.

When they arrived at the hotel, my friend paid for her room but instead of leaving her alone, the taxi driver entered the room with her. According to his statement, he had sat quietly in a chair in a corner of the room. After lots of round-and-about explanations, she stated that he had started touching her breasts and trying to take off her pants. When she said no, he simply tried a bit harder. She eventually managed to convince him that this was not a good idea. She connected to the hotel's Wi-Fi and called me.

After an experience like that, you might expect me to argue that women shouldn't travel Latin America – and especially, not alone. If Argentina is presumed to be one of the safest countries in the region, and this can happen to a completely normal young woman, what could happen in other countries that are considered more dangerous? But I don't argue that. I believe women should travel alone in Latin America.

This experience shook me very deeply. I have been traveling on my own since I was eighteen, and never has anything like that happened to me. I lived on my own in Spain, I studied in Cuba without access to the Internet, and I traveled alone in Colombia. I have never been robbed, never been mugged, and never been abused. This was a wake-up call for me.

I believe an experience like this proves that we – as women – need to consider that we are moving around in another context, another culture and another reality when we travel Latin America. We must make an active choice about how we behave. We shouldn't be afraid, but we should be aware that these things do happen, across the region, and even though abuse is never the woman's fault, of course, there are some things we can do to ensure we travel more safely. We need to take care of one another, share our stories and learn how best to cope.

When traveling, it is okay from time to time to be skeptical. It is okay to be distrustful. It is okay not to talk to everybody who wants to talk to you, and it is okay to refuse the offer of a free drive or a homemade beer.

It is okay to be a strong-minded, tough woman – and a strong-minded, tough woman who says no.

Rebecca Hoffmann

Rebecca is Danish but has fallen in love with Latin America. She studied Spanish in Cuba for four months and traveled around Colombia alone. Even though her looks and attitude tend to stand out (tall, blonde and strong-minded) she decided her international undergraduate program with Spanish was not enough, so she moved to Argentina for her Masters. You are now most likely to find this Viking-turned-Latina strolling the streets of Buenos Aires. Rebecca shares her stories about Latin America, and Buenos Aires in particular, at *Becci Abroad* (www.becci.dk). You can follow her on Twitter and Instagram: @becciabroad.

Could this be the Place?

Julia Buschmann

The high grasses sway in the breeze, up and down, up and down, like waves running through a green sea. Cotton-ball clouds project shadows onto the grass that travel in dramatic shapes across the land, alternatingly dimming and lighting the scene of two horsemen crossing a lush savannah. From far the snort of one of their horses is heard, then the lowing of cattle from somewhere in the distance. The whistling of a heron travels past, rapidly ascending in volume, reaching its peak and descending again as the bird vanishes from sight. Another horse snort seems to answer the bird.

Then silence falls over the prairie, the two figures almost melding with the grass in the shimmering heat. The horses' steps smack in the partly flooded savannah, a rhythmic squelching of hooves treading through mud and water. The humid air is heavy with the vapours of horse sweat, warm leather and heated silt. The horses throw their heads up to banish the flies that buzz around them. The flies are thirsty for the fluids from the horses' eyes and nostrils, and keen to lay their eggs in their ears. These warm shells offer safety in an otherwise harsh environment, where temperatures suddenly drop at night and large numbers of birds hunt for even larger numbers of insects. The horses seem to get idler with every period of hot sun, their necks longer and their eyes more closed. The horsemen have been riding for most of the morning and the sun will soon be at its highest. It is time for a break and they head towards a luxuriant stretch of palm trees.

Slightly hunched, the horsemen sit under large *sombreros*, their backs rhythmically seesawing in unison with their horses' movements and their legs in jeans, stained with mud that is now drying to a crust. One is chewing on the end of a long stalk of grass.

That horseman is me. Not so much of a man, but a woman in her late twenties on a mission to bring an old childhood dream to life. I raise my head and squint my eyes, scanning the savannah for white-tailed deer and birds of prey. In the distance the prairie blends with the pale blue horizon. Sweat stings my eyes and I wipe my face with one end of the poncho that is slung around my neck to protect it from burning. The sun eagerly seeks to redden every square inch of bare skin it can get its rays on. I am guessing from the glowing heat in my cheeks that my face must have taken on the colour of overripe strawberries.

I hear the voices of a distant past I once called the present and for a brief moment I hear mocking laughter, too. Then it is superseded by the shrill cries of a couple of lapwings that we take by surprise. Their hysteric wailing cuts the silence and chases away the scornful voices of my past. The birds fly up frantically as if they have never encountered a human before, and perhaps they haven't. Soon the couple settles on the ground again a safe distance away, their necks stretched, their heads bobbing, casting us wary looks. Silence falls over the land again. Only the wind swishes the grasses and brushes the crowns of the palm trees that irregularly dot the savannah. The smell of horse reaches my nose and I settle back into the blissful doziness that comes from being carried. I don't mind the mud on my jeans, the sweat-soaked shirt that is stuck to my back or the glowing heat radiating from my cheeks to the tips of my ears. Gone are the voices from twenty years ago. Gone are the sneers.

Back then, I was a timid blonde child who had more imaginary friends than real ones. People would ask what I wanted to be when I grew up and the answer always caused much amusement at afternoon coffee parties, dinners and outings. "A cowboy," I said with my ears turning red. "Oh, you mean a farmer?" someone's father or mother would ask, causing one of the children to burst out laughing and infect everyone else in the room. Sometimes at home my mother would ask if I could not think of a more feminine career.

"Like what?"

"Well, anything, my dear."

"There are female farmers, Mum."

"You're right."

"And cowboys? Are there female cowboys?"

"I am not sure. Not many, I would imagine. You need to be strong to be a cowboy."

"I am!"

"I see."

It was my father who planted these ideas in my head. At least once a week there would be a cowboy movie on the telly and I was allowed to watch it with him. He would also take me on long walks through the forest and across muddy fields. We would build river dams in streams and whistle by blowing air past a blade of grass held between the palms of our hands. His proud face when I climbed to the top of the walnut tree in our garden or jumped into an algae infested pond without fear motivated me more than anything else. Perhaps it laid the foundation for a lifelong desire for nature and for the careless freedom to play in it.

I had no clear idea of what a cowboy did, of course. All I could see at age nine or ten was someone on horseback, riding free in vast landscapes and looking rather dashing in boots and a hat. Did these extensive sceneries in movies even exist in real life? Did cowboys exist? And if they did not, then yes, perhaps becoming a farmer would be the closest thing.

Much later at university, while pursuing a masters rather than a career in farming, I met a Colombian. A boyish dark skinned chap who made me laugh, liked walking in the park and exploring new places, and who had a photo of himself on a white horse pinned to the wall above his desk. In the photo he wore a hat, jeans and no shoes. I could see palm trees in the background. "Are you a cowboy?" I asked and he laughed.

"I am a *llanero*."

"A what, sorry?"

"A *llanero*. I come from the Llanos, the prairies of Colombia."

For the next hours I hardly spoke, but listened with glowing eyes as each of his words painted a picture I had long forgotten about. He showed me photos of his family's farm and outlined the differences between various types of cattle. He played videos of men riding horses against backdrops of fiery red sunsets, palm trees and open grasslands that met the horizon. I watched video after video of magnificent horses cantering in slow motion, of men playing small guitars, lassoing cows and hollering. Much to my delight, there were even videos of women riding and lassoing. That night in a small room of a student residence in the northeast of England I learnt that Colombia was so much more than guerilla fighters and Shakira, the pop star. There and then Colombia became a land of cowboys, of virgin landscapes and inevitably a place of longing. Could this be the place to let those childhood dreams come true?

As is often the case, life got in the way of those dreams. I, perhaps unconsciously, followed other people's suggestions and landed a typical women's occupation in public relations. How often I would stand by the canteen window as my lunch box rotated around in the yellow light of the little microwave and gaze out across a world of concrete and buildings. The neat square patches of green in between were the only sign of natural life and from the eighth floor, they could not have looked more distant.

I would look around the room, at the white walls, the acrylic table tops, the beech wood chairs held together by chromed metal, plastic trays stapled neatly on the counter of yet another acrylic table top, hygienic metal boxes holding small packages of sugar and wooden sticks for stirring by the coffee machine. The machine was a towering apparatus with flashing lights behind various buttons; cappuccino, latte macchiato, café au lait, americano, espresso – a colourful assortment of coffee creations from around the world that simulate the purchaser's expression of individuality. Whether we pressed the latte macchiato-button or the café au lait-button on the machine, the outcome would look and taste exactly the same.

Very much like every workday in this building was a little bit different but somehow always tasted the same. And all this acrylic and white. Was there anything natural? Even the green apples in the fruit bowl on the counter looked artificial. A jubilant ping of the microwave would eventually order me back to duty. Eat, work, go home, repeat.

One afternoon I called a fly fisherman in Aberdeenshire to interview him as a potential ambassador for a campaign my team was working on. He told me that he had been out and about on the moors since dawn, lovely day, he assured me. He sounded happy and rosy-cheeked. I told him how much I would love to be there with him rather than in the office. I must have sounded woeful and pale. That same night I lay awake in bed and remembered with a pounding heart how I had roamed fields and forests as a girl and how much I loved the smell of it. If a man could be a fly fisherman and sound happy, then perhaps I could be a cowgirl and sound happy. And wasn't this the whole point of living anyway? Three months later I was on a flight to Colombia.

We reach the forest's cooling shade. The soundscape inside the grove is different. The noises of the savannah are dampened down and there is no wind that carries sounds from afar. Instead, the tread of our horses echo back at us from the surrounding green walls. A bird shrieks as if to announce our arrival. The rippling of a stream inside the forest reaches us and there is a collateral shuffling in the palm trees far above. We lead the horses towards the stream for a drink. Upon reaching the water we hear a loud splash nearby.

My pulse rises immediately. "An iguana," says Fernando.

"They can swim?"

"Yes."

"I had no idea."

"I had no idea," or more accurately, "*No sabía*," seems to be among the top sentences I have uttered since arriving in Colombia. Pineapples grow near the ground like crowns emerging from plants with long spiky leaves: *no sabía*. There are monkeys in the eastern plains of Colombia, plenty of them and various species: *no sabía*. Colombia has the greatest avian biodiversity in the world: *no sabía*. Travelling in Colombia actually does not feel nearly as dangerous as the media (and most people I know) have tried to suggest: *no sabía*. Colombia is a patchwork of different cultures, dialects and landscapes where people identify with a certain region first and as a Colombian second: *no sabía*.

We ride into the shallow clear water of the palm forest, called a gallery forest, Fernando explains to me. It forms a gallery following the course of the water like a green tape cutting through the otherwise rather plain savannah. "A typical element of the Llanos ecosystem," Fernando says. Ha! *No sabía*! I almost want to shout with joy and clap my hands, so exciting and different and exotic is all this. I take a deep breath of jungle air and hide a goofy grin.

We loosen the reigns of our horses so they can drink from the stream. Looking up into the green roof we listen to their gulps with rapt attention. How peaceful it is, I want to think, before the high-pitched whirring of a mosquito gets annoyingly close to my ear. I lash out. "We better get out of the forest," says Fernando. "*Perdón?*" I ask. I find it hard to adjust to the fast mumbling sounds of Colombia's Orinoco region, not that my Spanish is especially proficient anyway. Mouths hardly open, the locals speak in rapid prosody, dispense with much of the intonation and gestures that could provide helpful clues and throw in hyper-local expressions that are unintelligible, even to other Colombians.

I follow Fernando across the forest. A bird melancholically sings, a Colombian cuckoo perhaps? A play of shadows and sunlight dances on the forest floor. I study Fernando stealthily from behind, watching how he dips in and out of the shade as the horse carries him. He wears jeans rolled up above leathery dark feet in a light mud crust, a knife kept in a cowhide case on his belt, a dirty white shirt that forms a horizontal wrinkle at his lower back and a black hat, perhaps of felt or leather but I cannot be sure. His upper body bobs naturally from left to right to left with every step of his horse, like he was born to do just that. I am alone in the Colombian jungle with a man I don't know and whom I can barely understand. A thrill rises from the area of my stomach, a sense of adventure I had long needed.

"You going to Colombia," an acquaintance had said in a disapproving tone. "This worries me."

"What? Why?" I asked.

He was grateful for the interruption that saved him from saying what he was thinking. A European woman alone, a woman of your petite figure, fragile and naïve, it could only be a terrible mistake. His eyes had wandered down my body and back up for a split second. It was enough to infuriate me and make me want to go more than ever. The comments I faced after I announced the news ranged from an approving "Wow, amazing" to a wary "Ooh, not many positive things I hear coming out of Colombia" to an ignorant "Colombia? Like Brazil?"

Latin America in general and Colombia in particular seems to provoke mixed feelings. Colombia has the sound of danger to it, a notorious reputation. Even more so, who knew the Llanos? Who knew there were cowboys in Colombia and prairies, when it was known for its guerilla-infested jungles and mountains, cocaine plantations and kidnappings of tourists, unionists, journalists, expats and pretty much any other civilian. And if this was not enough to prevent foreigners from visiting, then perhaps the general delinquencies would; petty crimes, assaults, corrupt policemen and the abuse of tourists as clueless 'mules', drug couriers, upon leaving the country.

"We used to pay the *vacuna* along this route," the driver had told me on the way to the farm when I asked about security in the Llanos. At first I had not understood what he meant as my brain always seemed to need a few moments to process Spanish. Then I got it. They had paid protection money. "And today?"

"*No, señora,*" he assures me. Then he adds, after a glance at my thoughtful face in the rear mirror, "Don't you worry." He smiles now. I will experience many deja-vu moments of this throughout my Colombian trip. "Don't you worry," seems to be a national claim, and "used to" a state the country is in now. It used to be dangerous, critical, problematic. We used to pay the *vacuna*, used to lose family members to conflict, used to be scared. Now there is James Rodriguez, the football star, there is Nairo Quintana, the world-class cyclist, and there is still Shakira.

We reach the other end of the forest, then open savannah again. The sun is at its highest point. We stay in the forest shade and dismount. Fernando shyly passes me a package wrapped in a leaf. I open it to find plantain crisps, dried meat, and some little pastries. We eat silently, the savannah before us, the forest at our backs. The horses chew steadily on the grass. I cast a look at Fernando, he pretends not to notice. Politely, he had saddled up the horses in the morning. He had accompanied me and talked and explained whenever there was something to explain or talk about. He treated me with more respect than I was used to and, since reaching the Llanos, I felt like I was onto something when it comes to how women are treated in Colombia, and perhaps in the Llanos in particular.

Later that day we come to a farmhouse and a resolute woman with a brown hat and rolled up sleeves helps me dismount, holding out a small but sturdy hand to greet me with an affectionate smile. "Carmensa," she says and I look into her steel-blue eyes framed by laughter lines.

"Doña Carmensa is the administrator of this ranch," Fernando tells me.

"Is that so?" I turn towards her with an acknowledging expression.

"She manages six men and their families and one thousand eight hundred cattle," Fernando adds, visibly pleased that he can impress me yet again.

"Doña Carmensa, how do you assert yourself in a man's world?" I ask, immediately regretting how pathetic the question sounds. She doesn't seem to mind and laughs with pride. That evening I learn all I needed to learn about *llaneras*. Sturdy women, willful, hard-working, independent, not afraid to start an argument – in fact, in favour of arguing – and just as resolute, if not more so, than most men.

I don't recall the last time I felt as content and as tired as I do that night. Swaying in my hammock under the mosquito net, listening to the orchestra of crickets and frogs and nighthawks, I dare to dream again. The vast landscapes within reach, the cattle and horses, the cowboys and cowgirls, the freedom and adventure, all laid out before me, longing for me as much as I have been longing for them.

Julia Buschmann

Julia travelled, studied, and worked in various countries before following her curiosity to Colombia in 2014. She has since learned to get up before sunrise, lasso horses, and has developed a keen interest in the wildlife of Colombia's eastern plains where she lives at the foot of the Andes with her husband and their three cats. Fuelled by Colombian coffee, the country's magical realism, and a desire to introduce as many people as possible to Colombia's natural wonders and great experiences, she co-founded the eco-tourism business www.aventurecotours.com and records her stories and adventures on www.buschpost.com. Born and raised in Germany near the Dutch border, Julia still enjoys riding her bicycle, sipping white wine, and having a good old cake and coffee get-together.

Gunfire in the Night

Kelly Symonds

I arrived in Mexico City on December 21, 1997. I was twenty-two. The day after I arrived, the Acteal Massacre in the Chiapas region occurred. Forty-five indigenous Tzotzil were killed; twenty-one women, fifteen children and nine men. The massacre was horrific and shocked the nation. It caused international outrage and the whole of Mexico felt like it was on the verge of an uprising or revolution. Those killed were Roman Catholic advocates from a pacifist group called Las Abejas (The Bees), who denounced violence and protested through peaceful demonstrations.

It is rumoured that Las Abejas supported the Zapatista army. I had heard a lot about the Zapatista rebels, a revolutionary political and militant faction. Many sympathised with these alleged freedom fighters and they were often hailed as heroes because they sought indigenous control over their land and local resources. As a result of the slaughter, President Ernesto Zedillo ordered an investigation into the massacre. The paramilitary killers were indigenous Indians who lived in a neighbouring village. They were members of the PRI, the Institutional Revolutionary Party, who had alleged connections to the government. Prosecutors later found that government officials, local police and soldiers at a nearby military outpost, failed to intervene during the attack, thereby allowing the carnage to continue for several hours. The controversy over the massacre and its aftermath continues to this day.

Two weeks after my arrival, I took a night bus from Tuxtla

Gutiérrez to Palenque to visit the Mayan ruins in the Chiapas region. The area was the base of the Zapatista rebels and had been volatile since the massacre. Both the Zapatistas and the paramilitaries were active; stealing and looting to fund their operations. There were many reported incidents of rape and assault; an American tourist had been raped just a few days earlier. This particular route could only be travelled at night.

I was studying Cultural Studies at university, and was constantly engrossed in conversations with other travellers and young Mexicans about the country's political struggles. I was enchanted by Mexico's mysterious Mayan and Aztec archaeology and its vibrant and diverse landscapes, so even though I understood it was a dangerous time to take an overnight bus, that danger still felt like it was a million miles away.

The bus was full of indigenous Mexicans, mostly families, although I did notice a Western couple sitting at the back. I sat next to an old indigenous man whose piercing green eyes sunk into his dark, wrinkled complexion. He wore a cowboy hat, a checked shirt, jeans and cowboy boots. He smelt old too; a musky, muddy smell mixed with sweat and tobacco. I nodded at him and he smiled. I was tired so I pulled my cap over my face and closed my eyes.

I awoke to several loud explosions and the sound of breaking glass. It felt like the bus had hit something and the windscreen had smashed. The bus stopped. The lights went out and some of the women began to scream. The lights came on and I saw the confusion and the fright on the other passengers' faces. Had a tyre burst? The old man next to me made the sign of the cross. He looked both baffled and petrified.

The doors flung open and two men wearing army fatigues entered the bus. They were carrying automatic rifles. They were either a paramilitary group or the Zapatistas, I couldn't tell which. The men were terrifying, they had ski masks covering their faces and they were shouting. The old man began to cry.

I heard the sound of automatic machine gun fire from outside and realised the two men on the bus were not alone. It took me a few seconds to assess the danger. I was a lone foreigner and I could not speak Spanish. I had a lot of cash and hundreds of pounds worth of travellers cheques stashed in the money belt around my waist. I was so scared I felt almost unable to move. I pulled my cap back over my face and pretended to be asleep.

The two men begin to search and rob everyone onboard. I discovered later that they had forced each passenger to stand up and remove what they had in their pockets. One of the armed men, who seemed to be in charge, hit a man adjacent to me on the head with the butt of his rifle. I heard the thud and my whole body tensed. I could hear the men rifle through handbags, backpacks, and wallets and was told that they threw all items of value into a large sack. They were leaving nothing behind. This was a bus full of families. No one was going to play the hero.

I heard the men work their way down the left-hand side of the bus. When they yelled at the couple behind me, my brain switched into gear and adrenaline began to pump through my veins. I realised I had done nothing to secure my belongings. My body had shut down in fear. I could have tried to remove my money belt and hidden it down the side of my seat, but it was too late now. I pretended to be asleep. I just wanted it to be over.

The men shouted at the old man. I continued to lean my head against the window with my cap over my face. The next thing I knew, one of the men had knocked the cap off my head. He looked shocked to see a young, white woman staring back at him. My cap had hidden my face and blond hair.

He began to scream at me. It seemed I had made him angrier by pretending to be asleep, as if anyone could have slept through all that. In panic, I picked up my backpack, which lay at my feet and searched for anything of value. My hands shook as I offered him my purse and camera. He took both, but then he threw the camera back at me. I waited for him to tell me to stand up so he could search my body as he had done with everyone else. But he moved onto the couple in front of me, whom he forced to stand up so he could search them thoroughly.

The other man went to the entrance of the bus and shouted at his comrades outside. They shouted something in response. It felt like there was a sudden sense of urgency. The man by the entrance shouted at his companion, as if urging him to hurry, and then both men were gone.

It took about thirty seconds for the people around me to react to what had happened. Several passengers began to wail. It felt like the whole bus gave a sigh of relief but entered into hysteria at the same time. Some passengers began to shout at the driver. I assumed they were telling him to drive away.

The engine started after a few failed attempts but the driver seemed to be finding it difficult to get the bus into gear. There was a horrendous grinding noise. The bus crept forward for perhaps a minute and then the engine died. The driver tried to start it, over and over, but nothing happened. Finally, he stood up and seemed to be telling us that he had to investigate the problem. He was clearly shaken and afraid to leave the bus. A couple of men rose from their seats, despite obvious protests from their wives, and walked down the bus so they could help the driver. He opened the doors and they stepped down together. We weren't five hundred metres from where the incident had taken place.

There was a low hum of chatter and I saw that some people were crying. I looked around and saw the two foreigners at the back of the bus. They appeared to be unharmed. There was another man with a bloody gash on his head, where he had been hit with the butt of the rifle. The couple behind him was examining his wound. There was a second man on my side of the aisle, a few seats back, and he was injured too. His wife was dabbing at his wound with a cloth. Most of the passengers appeared to be comforting one another. Wives were consoled by their husbands and children were rocked by their mothers.

The old man beside me looked directly into my eyes and then he patted my hand. It was such a simple gesture that I couldn't stop the tears from forming in my eyes. I smiled at him.

My hands were still shaking. I needed to smoke a cigarette to calm my nerves and I had a strong desire to talk to someone about what had happened. I stepped outside the bus.

A young Mexican couple came towards me as I lit my cigarette. The man began to speak in rapid Spanish.

"I don't speak Spanish," I interjected.

"Are you okay?" he said in English, with a thick accent.

"Yes, I'm fine, thank you," I replied, amazed and relieved that we could communicate.

"I'm sorry about what happened," he said.

"Who were those men?"

"I think it was the Zapatistas. This area is very dangerous at the moment, you should not travel at night."

The man was considerate and so concerned for my welfare that I began to feel embarrassed that I had taken such a risk. Relief filled my body and I wanted to hug them both.

I looked at the bus. The foreign couple had now disembarked and were heading straight towards me.

"Are you okay?" I said, as they approached.

"Yes. Man, that was the scariest thing I've ever been through," the man said. The woman was very pale.

"Did they do anything to you?" she said.

"They took my wallet, fifty pesos, that's it."

"You're lucky, the guy in front of us was knocked out, he needs to go to a hospital. One of the men groped me. I was so scared that they would do something else but, thank God, he just grabbed my tits. I was terrified Tim would try to stop them."

She looked at her boyfriend. He frowned.

"They took our wallets with our cash and our credit cards," she said. "Luckily, we always keep spare money in our big backpacks, and we've got travellers cheques. But they took about US$200."

"They didn't even search me," I said.

"We were worried about you because we knew you were on your own," the woman said. "We've been hearing bad stories about girls travelling alone recently."

I knew what she meant and I didn't want to imagine what could have happened. Those thoughts had already raced through my brain and I realised I had felt more shaken thinking about what hadn't happened, than what had. I finished my cigarette and lit a second one.

"Do you know what's happening to the bus?" I said.

"Yeah," said Tim. "The Zapatistas pushed rocks across the road to form a barrier, the driver didn't see the rocks and drove into them, smashing the window and the engine. Now we have to wait for another bus to come and collect us. The driver has radioed his company and the bus is on its way."

"We have to wait until then? What if they come back? I'm sure they're watching us now," I cried.

"I have the same feeling," Tim replied.

"You're crazy travelling on your own," the woman said.

I hate it when people say that. I looked at the bus and saw several passengers walking towards us.

"I'm not alone," I said. "Look."

The passengers gathered around us, clearly concerned for our safety. I was touched. After a short while, I made my excuses so I could climb back onto the deserted bus and sit for a few moments alone. I was no longer scared. I was in awe of the other passengers' kindness and the fact we were the ones they wanted to reassure.

Kelly Symonds

Kelly's first trip outside of the United Kingdom was a year spent travelling Southeast Asia and Australia when she was seventeen, which cemented her love for distant places. With eight years' experience as a TV director (including three years at MTV) under her belt, Kelly continued to travel extensively. She trained as an English teacher and taught in Thailand, Ecuador, and Brazil before returning to England to complete her Masters in Social Work. Four years of frontline children's social work and a looming fortieth birthday later, Kelly hopped on a plane to Rio de Janeiro, Brazil, where she planned to find a hubby and lap up the sunshine on Ipanema beach. The husband is a work in progress but, in the meantime, Kelly is writing her first book, teaching English to pay the bills, and soaking up that sun.

You're Never Too Old

April Wood

I'm writing this in a bus station in Medellín, Colombia, as I wait for an overnight bus to Cartagena. I am halfway through my second solo trip to South America, this time nine weeks in Ecuador and Colombia and then into Central America for Panama and Costa Rica. My first trip, at the age of seventy-eight, was in 2013 for twelve weeks and covered Brazil, Uruguay, Argentina and Chile.

I have such wonderful memories of that trip. Generally due to the kindness and consideration of the people, and without exception their surprise to discover I'm from England. It seems few visitors from my country venture outside the tourist spots and meet the people of South America. They always smile and apologise for their poor English (your reply of, "You're doing very well, where did you learn it?" will have them running around in circles trying to please you).

So many small kindnesses, too many to mention – and many larger ones too; like the hostel owner in Valparaíso, Chile, who insisted on sending a taxi to the bus terminal for me and ensured I saw the most interesting parts of the city. And the box office in Manaus Opera House in Brazil who, on the opening night of the opera season, miraculously found me a perfect seat for a wonderful performance of Janacek's *The Cunning Little Vixens*. They charged me next to nothing because I was a visitor.

My seventy-ninth birthday was spent travelling over the Andes Mountains from San Pedro de Atacama, Chile, to Salta, Argentina. When the bus conductor, on checking my passport, discovered it was my birthday, he flung his arms around me and hugged me, shouting to the other passengers, "It's her birthday!" whereupon everyone clapped. You're never too old to travel. It's a "can do" attitude of mind.

My tips for travelling? Always be alert, dress modestly and I make it a rule, no alcohol whilst travelling. Don't look wealthy – dress down. Never wear any jewellery, walk purposefully even if you're not too sure where you're going, and keep that map and phone hidden – try to memorise your route. Likewise, keep your camera concealed but handy for that great photo moment.

Would I go back for a third visit? Of course I would. Travel is a wonderful thing; it broadens the mind and enriches the spirit, and always teaches you something new.

Age means nothing. Just let those itchy feet keep you travelling.

April Wood

April calls London, England, home, but has lived in several countries including Greece, where she taught English and crewed yachts around the islands, and Turkey, where she worked as a governess. April found living in the USA rather bland, so she took up flying and piloted two-and-four-seater aircraft. She lived in Sri Lanka and South Africa and has travelled widely, mostly trekking and camping. April paints in oils and pastels, attends dance classes, and has a great interest in all of the arts, including drama and classical music. She is now preparing for a new career in motivational speaking.

The Uninvited Visitor

Allison Yates

The first thing I remember that Sunday morning was the feeling of dread. Dread, because of exactly what it meant. Tonsillitis. The inevitable blisters were growing rapidly by the minute, constricting my throat and causing pulsating waves of pain down to my toes when I tried to swallow. It meant the end of my trip to Havana as I knew it.

"Allison?" asked my friend, Kimberly, just above the volume of a whisper. She peeked her head through the doorway of my room and walked closer to the bed. I wasn't exactly asleep, but I wasn't fully conscious, either. I was vacillating between the blurred lines of fever-induced dreams, of stick arms attached to cars and my friends with balloons for faces, and the reality of the tickling breeze from the open window, the yellow light reflecting off the white walls, my sweat-drenched bed sheets clinging to me and the subtle shouts of conversations in Parque Cristo below. The dread was sitting next to me and invading my space.

"Do you want to come with us to Varadero?" she asked. I hadn't been feeling well the day before, either. Magdalena, the woman who lived in the apartment below us and who had rented us this apartment, had brought up ibuprofen and some other tablets. The assumption was that if I woke up improved, I'd go to the beach with Kimberly, her boyfriend Moisés, and Hannah, another friend. If not, I'd stay back and rest.

"No," I could barely say without jolts of pain.

She left thinking I'd be better by the time she got back. I

knew I wasn't going to get better. I had suffered tonsillitis too many times to think that at this stage, without antibiotics, I would improve. But I couldn't find the strength or will to take the steps I should have taken the day before, to find a doctor and get on antibiotics.

A few minutes later I heard Kimberly and Moisés talking, followed by the door shutting. I glided back into the fantastical stupor of a high fever, hearing salsa rhythms and tail ends of conversations creeping through the window. That would be my only contact today. I was alone.

I figured out early on that, contrary to what some people believe, Latin America is more than just a place of violent dictatorships, kidnappings, and drug wars. I'm not naïve enough to think that such tragedies don't happen, but I am wise enough to know that those stories do not define a region.

I've studied in Argentina, volunteered multiple times in Panama and traveled to almost every country in South America. Whether transiting overnight from Ecuador to Colombia, getting lost in the fields of a province of Buenos Aires trying to find a country house, or driving along the coast of Puerto Rico, people have been enormously kind to me. It is these same people that often stop to warn me of the danger of others, perhaps not recognizing that those 'others' are often genuinely compassionate people much like themselves.

A few months before, I had flown into Buenos Aires on a budget flight that landed at two o'clock in the morning. I took a taxi to my friend's house. In the rush to gather my bags and run up to my friend's apartment in the eeriness of Microcentro at night, my black wallet fell out of my purse and into the darkness of the cab.

About a half hour after settling in, I realized my wallet was missing. Cursing myself for my stupidity – I had a credit card, two debit cards and US$100 cash inside – I frantically called the taxi company. My friend mentioned something about opportunistic *porteños*, noting that something lost is not often returned.

"My name is Allison, and I lost my wallet in one of your cabs," I explained, trying to hide my pessimism at the possibility of it being recuperated. "Oh, of course. Your driver already called. He noticed it when he got home and cleaned out his car. He has it," the operator said, and gave us his number.

The next day, the driver came back to the city on his day off and hand delivered my wallet. A credit card, two debit cards and US$100 cash, all intact.

"*No lo puedo creer,*" said my friend. I can't believe it. "People are good!" he cheered.

Such examples have colored my experience of Latin America, proving this continent is full of people with principles and compassion. I knew that those people went to great lengths for others, but it wasn't until I got sick in Cuba that I realized to what extent strangers could care for me.

By about eleven o'clock, instead of the improvement my friends had expected when they left three hours earlier, my condition was only worsening. My dread was gone and had turned to sadness. Tonsillitis wasn't on its way, it was here. I felt truly alone, tossing and turning in stale and damp sheets on a stiff Cuban mattress.

I was lying awake on the twin bed with my eyes closed, listening to the repeated buzz of the fan above me, when I heard the shuffle of slippers against the tile floor. I opened my eyes and saw Magdalena, a petite seventy year-old woman with inflamed joints and painted-on eyebrows, in the doorway.

Her daily visits had irritated me the past few days. I hadn't liked her unexpected arrivals when my friends and I were walking around in our underwear or getting ready to leave. She would let herself in uninvited to calculate how many of the provided waters or Havana Club rum bottles we had drunk so she could update our tab.

But today, she was my lifeline. I was grateful for the lack of privacy. I didn't have the strength to get out of bed except to reach the toilet, and without Wi-Fi I felt isolated from any assistance. In between thinking about what I would miss during my last two days in Cuba I had been listening to the same pre-loaded podcasts over and over.

I was about to discover that the invasion of the privacy of others comes with a deep commitment to them. Knowing whatever ailments or suffering the neighbor is experiencing creates a sense of responsibility for their wellbeing. In contrast to the isolation of the acre lots in the neighborhood where I grew up in the Midwestern United States, in Cuba physical proximity seemed to generate a shared experience, for good or for bad.

"Oh, Magdalena!" I wailed, "I feel horrible. I need help." Magdalena had a bunch of her own problems. A pinched nerve. Back aches. Labored breathing. Difficulty climbing stairs. That day, she pretended that none of those existed.

First, Magdalena called two of her doctor friends. Since going to the clinic would cost me at least US$70, she said, she preferred that her friends came to me. It was Sunday, but the couple came. They prescribed antibiotics and ran to fill the prescription for me: US$3. Meanwhile, Magdalena sat next to them, filling them in about what I couldn't communicate and taking mental notes on my recovery.

Magdalena got her son to come and stock the fridge full of water bottles. She came back up with a salt gargle and more ibuprofen and told me to wait a few minutes before I took the antibiotics. Then, she brought up chicken stew she had made into puree so I could easily swallow it. Cassava, chicken, potatoes all smashed to be easily ingested.

Magdalena came back several more times to check on me, reminding me she was just below. Did I need anything? How did I feel? Were the antibiotics working? It wasn't just Magdalena who was concerned.

By the afternoon, everybody in the apartment block seemed to realize I wasn't well. Magdalena's son brought me liquid yogurt. Her husband came up to wish me well. Richard, the neighbor, came into my room to see that I was alive, and later

Magdalena's daughter-in-law brought me a beef stew.

I had stayed in my twin bed all day, hearing snatches of car engines, speakers and bicycle taxi horns sneak through the windows. The outside world felt distant, but I wasn't abandoned. The day turned to dusk and the light from yellow to pink. The air cooled as my fever subsided. Getting sick in Cuba didn't mean losing contact with others or falling into a deep sickness alone.

Magdalena was renting her apartment to us, but that day she didn't take the role of landlady. She was, instead, a mother, refusing to let me pay for the meals or medicine she brought me and spending her day worried about my well-being.

Later that evening, Magdalena came up once more before she went to bed. She sat opposite me on the other bed, her frail fingers grasping the sides of the mattress. I told her I was much better. The antibiotics were starting to kick in, and I was even able to walk around the apartment without feeling winded.

"My daughter lives in England," she told me, her eyes distant yet concentrated on me. "She broke her arm and can't work. And there, there's no one to care for her."

She looked deeply worried. Her daughter was so far away. Without funds or resources to care for her, she was stuck on the other side of the ocean, only praying someone could help her daughter. She wasn't going to let the same thing happen to me.

Allison Yates

Allison is a writer and traveler who loves *cumbia*, coconut water, and the Spanish language. After she graduated from Indiana University, USA, she lived, worked, and traveled in Europe, Asia and Australia, but her heart has always belonged to Latin America. Allison lives for funny conversations and hilarious situations, like the times she couchsurfed with a Pitbull look-alike in the Basque Country, Spain, or worked on a uranium mine in Australia. Follow Allison's writing and travels on Instagram: @allisonyateswrites.

Look at my Life Now

Rebecca Roach

Giving my notice at work was one of the most invigorating moments of my life. I had a comfortable job and salary, but I was continuously asked to do more with less until I started to feel more like a number than a valued employee. I realized I needed a break from the corporate world and I wanted some excitement. I had always wanted to make my way back to South America, after studying abroad there in college.

A friend of mine had volunteered as an English teacher in Chile and I asked her about the program. I wrestled with the idea of applying for several weeks. "Am I actually going to quit my job to teach English in Chile?" No matter how many times my fear told me to remain comfortable, I couldn't shake the gut feeling that this was something I should do. My final push to apply came after my father passed away unexpectedly.

I say unexpectedly because it was sudden, but the way my dad abused his body over the years made it not so unexpected. He had long battled addictions to both alcohol and smoking. I knew, deep down, that the day would come prematurely for him but nothing can ever prepare you for losing a parent.

It's a gaping hole. A finality that changes you immediately. You don't realize the impact a parent has on you until they're gone. Until you pick up the phone to call your dad and realize you can't. Until you imagine the day you get married and he won't be there to walk you down the aisle. Until you realize all the things he will miss about this world and your life. Until you worry about forgetting the memories you shared with him, or his voice, or how he walked or what his laugh sounded like.

Clinging to memories is like trying to keep sand in your hands. You want to ensure that not even a tiny piece is forgotten.

Experiencing that loss lit a fire in me. I wasn't going to wait for the right moment to return to South America; I was going to create that moment. My dad and I had talked about it briefly. I remember him being a bit taken aback but ultimately supportive. He was usually supportive because he trusted me. That is one thing I will always be grateful for. He told me two things: how proud he was of me and that he trusted my judgment. It's something that instilled a lot of confidence in me.

I gave my company ten weeks' notice, sold or donated most of my belongings and put the rest into storage. My plan was to teach for a semester, travel for a while, and then the rest was up to me. I was purposely leaving my life open ended.

As I boarded my flight I couldn't help but hear the Whitesnake song lyrics, "Here I go again on my own," in my head. I know it's cheesy but it put a pep in my step. I was uprooting my life, putting myself in a new country, living with a family who could not speak English, and starting a new profession with just a week of training. Ready, set, holy shit I'm going.

I was soon on an overnight bus to my new home in Valdivia. I was excited to practice my Spanish but I knew Chileans spoke quickly and used a lot of slang, known as *chilenismos*. I was confident that with time and practice, I would get my bearings and be fine. And then I met my host grandpa.

My host grandpa spoke to me like he would with a Chilean. I tried to converse with him but I could not keep up. He kept talking while I stared at him. My eyes were wide and I was frozen by how little I understood. "Oh no," I thought. "Please don't cry." Within minutes, I was crying.

I knew there would be low moments. I just didn't know they would begin on day one. What most of us don't realize until we learn a new language is that when we're fluent, especially in our mother tongue, we speak really quickly.

Chileans speak extra quickly. It had been seven years since I had studied abroad and practiced my Spanish, and I didn't understand a thing this man was saying. Add to that the fact I had just moved out of my apartment, said goodbye to every person and comfort I loved, and walked into a stranger's house where I would be living for the next four months. It was overwhelming, and hardly the best start.

Here's the funny thing though. Once I calmed down, I started to understand some of what my host grandpa was saying. He graciously offered me a cup of tea (Chileans drink a lot of tea or *tecitos*) and we began to talk. I pulled out my dictionary, asked him to speak a little slower and gradually began to make out what he was saying. If I had retreated to my room, I would have been defeated. Instead, I stayed, and in the end we were able to converse. It was an important lesson that if I quit at the first sign of resistance or fear, I would never know how much I could achieve.

Before I knew it, I was wrapping up my semester and packing my bags for Patagonia, the first stop on my three-month travel plan. A few other volunteers and I had decided to hike the W trail in Torres del Paine National Park. I was happy to start my travels with a few familiar faces, before I broke off on my own.

The park is a wondrous place. Around every bend and corner there seemed to be a new mountain, lake, glacier or river to admire. But the five-day hike was more challenging than I expected, and it had its twists and turns.

By early morning on day two I was holding back tears. It was my first backpacking trip and I was hiking with two other volunteers who were avid hikers and trying to match their pace. We were climbing a steep hill when I started to doubt whether I could complete the hike. A few tears escaped and rolled down my cheek as I took yet another break. I confided in one of the others but did my best to hide the fact I was frustrated, because I was ashamed. I felt I was holding them all back.

I could hear my dad's voice in my head. Whenever I had struggled with something, no matter what it was, I would go to him for advice. Even though I wished I could hear it from him directly, I imagined what he would have said. "Well, how could you expect to be an expert on day one? You've never done this before. If you weren't nervous or frustrated, you wouldn't be human." My dad had a good way of reminding me not to be too hard on myself.

Two days later, I was consoling one of my friends. She was crying on the dusty ground, having lost her footing, fallen down and scraped her knee. It was a role reversal and I realized how much more confidence I had already acquired.

The trail tested me in a way I had never experienced. It was just me and the path ahead. No cell phone reception, no Wi-Fi, camping every night, collecting water from streams and rivers, putting one foot in front of the other. It also gave me a sense of personal success I had never felt before.

Most of my past accomplishments revolved around education and professional development. Graduations, internships, scholarships and new jobs. While those accomplishments made me proud and still do, this was different. It was more personal. No one gave me an award for finishing that trail but I left a piece of my heart in Patagonia. When we walked out of the park on day five, I looked back on the towering mountain peaks and teal blue lakes with a huge smile of pride and satisfaction. I walked off that trail the same way I conquered it; one step at a time.

In El Chaltén, in Argentina, I hiked Mount Fitz Roy, which takes ten hours. I ate lunch alone at the top of the mountain, admiring the lakes and jutting towers. The hike was much quieter than Torres del Paine and I felt even more connected to nature, enjoying the serenity and time to myself.

In El Calafate, I hiked across the Perito Moreno glacier. Stretching as far as the eye could see, it's an awesome creation of nature. The hike was rainy and cold but it was a once in a lifetime experience. The cherry on top was a celebratory whisky on the rocks, with ice freshly hacked from the glacier.

I continued to Buenos Aires and explored the city on foot, eating passion fruit cheesecake and sipping coffee while writing in my journal. I saw the philharmonic orchestra at Teatro Colón and spent New Year's Eve at the only bar in town showing Ohio State, my alma mater, playing in the National College Football Championship. I went to Parque Nacional Iguazu and marveled at the maze of waterfalls. I went to Mendoza, rented a bike and toured the wineries. I spent two weeks in rural Argentina, living on a farm and building sustainable housing.

I hiked Huayna Picchu at Machu Picchu in Peru and had some of the best ceviche in my life in Aguas Calientes. Now, as I wrap up my second semester of teaching in Chile, I am preparing for more travels throughout Chile, Bolivia, and Colombia. I eagerly await the stories I know are sure to come.

I had received a few incredulous stares and questions as I prepared to leave for Chile. "You're going by yourself? Do you know anyone down there? Is it safe?" Sometimes that came from co-workers, other times from acquaintances or members of my own family, although my closest friends and family always gave me their love and support. They trusted I had a brain that would help me navigate as best I could. I still experienced the bewildered "How could you possibly travel alone?" looks though. It's frustrating because I wonder how a man would be treated. I'm sure he would receive the same admiring looks I received. But would he receive the same level of questioning or warnings about whether he would be safe?

Luckily for me, my dad always built me up by saying how proud I made him. The thought that I was putting myself in danger never even crossed my mind. I was mostly just afraid of the uncharted territory and bucking the status quo. Now I look at all the things I would have missed had I not listened to that little voice inside me that urged me to go for it. What a far less interesting person I would have become.

I encourage as many people as I can to push through that fear. The worst thing that can happen is that you live with the regret of never having tried. The second worst thing is that you will have a terrible time, but I find that unlikely. The best thing is that you will forever be grateful you listened to that little voice inside your head that urged you to create your own adventure.

Throughout all of this, I have to thank my father. My world changed when he passed away, but in many ways it was for the better. As much as I want to have him back here on earth, to hear his voice again, to laugh with him, and hear his words of wisdom, I cannot help but appreciate the person I have become. I no longer wait for opportunities, I make them. Time is not guaranteed and I live my life to the fullest the best way I can.

Dad, thank you for continuing to shape me into the woman I am today even though you have left the physical life. Despite the fact that I'm almost thirty, I am still learning from you. Thank you for always telling me you were proud of me. I still gather strength from those words. Your Sweetie loves you and knows you are smiling with pride.

P.S. Can you believe my life right now?

Rebecca Roach

Rebecca proudly resides in her hometown of Cleveland, Ohio, USA, and insists it's a very cool place to live. She loves to sing but is aware others don't always enjoy listening to her. She's quite good at dancing and attributes that to her mother. In her free time Rebecca likes to crush her brothers at Mario Kart 64, play Bingo with her mother, and write in her journal at a local café (usually with coffee and a piece of cake). This was her first writing experience, and she now hopes to publish her own book about her travels in South America.

You can read more of Rebecca's writing on her blog, www.28tolifeblog.wordpress.com.

A Rugged Kinda Gal

Robin Verwest

There is only one road that travels the entire length of Baja California. It is narrow, with one lane in each direction, and paved to varying degrees. Named Mexican Federal Highway No 1, or Carretera Transpeninsular Benito Juarez, it runs from the top of Baja, at the U.S. border, to the southern tip, at Cabo San Lucas, just over a thousand miles away.

After crossing into Mexico, I caught a bus heading south. I asked the bus driver to drop me at a turnoff, where I would hitchhike to a hostel on the coast.

"Are you alone? Why are you not afraid?" asked the driver, a greasy, salivating, sweaty man, as he got my rucksack out of the bottom of the vehicle. He handed me my bags with what I can only guess must have been his most smouldering look and called, "You are very beautiful!" as I walked away to wait by the side of the road.

This was just one of many such experiences on my journey through Baja.

A fellow camper at Los Cerritos beach in Southern Baja told me about a great place to surf that was more suited to my ability level. He explained that there was no public transport for the final two hours of the journey, but that I would be able to get a ride without too much trouble.

On his advice, I packed fourteen litres of water into my backpack along with just enough clothes for my intended week-long trip. I left most of my belongings in La Paz. Later I learned that it was a misunderstanding: he had actually meant that while I would need plenty of water for the long, hot trip through the desert, I would not need water for the whole stay. I had planned to ration myself to two litres per day, wrongly thinking there would be no drinking water available. Lucky I'm strong, as it sure was a heavy load to carry.

I caught the dawn bus from La Paz to Ciudad Insurgentes, a town several hours north. From there, I walked up the road to the beginning of the highway and stuck my thumb out. I use the word highway very loosely – imagine sixty miles of tarmac with regular foot-deep craters, after which it became even worse.

First a guy stopped and said he was going as far as Zaragoza. I sized him up and reckoned I could handle him if necessary. He looked pretty harmless. He was vertically challenged, grossly overweight, and sported a large moustache. I got in. All the same, I did feel the need to make up a fictitious husband and children as we chatted in my rudimentary Spanish.

We passed through Zaragoza and continued driving through the desert, so I asked where he was going to drop me. He said he knew a good place just down the road where I would have a better chance of catching a ride. Eventually he pulled over on a stretch of broken road amongst the cacti under the midday sun. There he proceeded to masturbate while inviting me to help him out. Quite literally, he was a wanker. As quick as lightning, I leapt out of the car and grabbed my things. I tried to ignore him from the other side of the road, but by now he was also out of his car, still masturbating and shouting at me to, as he so eloquently put it, "come and shower under it." Finally, he finished himself off, got back in his car and drove off in the direction from which we had come. It was a relief to see him go, even if I was now totally alone in the middle of nowhere.

It was half an hour before another car appeared, and it drove straight past. When five *rancheros* in a pickup truck stopped a while later, I jumped in, thinking it couldn't get much worse. Luckily it didn't. The guys were great, they even gave me an icy beer to sip as I sat on the floor of the pickup. They dropped me in the shade of the only tree around, at a turnoff close to a house.

After that, I got a lift with a family and then another guy. He lifted his sunglasses and tried to dazzle me with his light green eyes. "All the women love my eyes," he told me. Somehow, I managed to restrain myself.

The turnoff for my destination was a little shrine by the side of the road, which was being used as a police checkpoint on that particular day. I waited there for three and a half hours for the next vehicle that was going my way. I passed the time with three policemen whose knowledge of the English language stopped at, "I love you," and "Come on, baby!" By the end of the afternoon, *los tres policías locos*, as I took to calling my new friends, all wanted to marry me, be my boyfriend, kiss me, or go disco dancing, which I now realise was quite ludicrous because there was no disco for at least two hundred miles.

At one point the officers asked me which of the three of them was the most handsome. "None of you," I replied, "You're all ugly." When they expressed an interest in learning some more English I taught them how to say, "You are an ugly, lazy, no-good policeman." Though I explained to them what this meant, they didn't seem to mind and repeated it to each other over and over again, laughing heartily amongst themselves each time. So keen was I to get away that when a car eventually pulled up, I practically hurled myself and my bag into the back.

After spending twelve hours on what should have been a six-hour car journey, I finally arrived at the beach. Someone kindly lent me a surfboard and I was able to catch a couple of waves before dark. I'd never experienced waves that I could ride for such a long distance before, and it was a fabulous way to end a rather trying day.

It's curious to think that the day before I set out on this journey, I went to a barbeque in the United States where people told me I was going to be raped, murdered, kidnapped, robbed or shot. I'm lucky I don't listen to fear mongers. That first ride was the only time I have ever felt unsafe or threatened in the past seven years I have spent in Mexico.

Being a lone traveller has made it far easier for others to approach and get to know me, and as a result I have made many new and lasting friendships. I travel light and love to sleep in my tent, take public transport and walk long distances. I will occasionally hitchhike when there is no other alternative. I have the confidence that comes from years of martial arts training in England, Thailand and Japan and I know I can protect myself, which opens the door for me to head out into the unknown.

Back on the beach, as the light dwindled, I pitched my tent on the sand right where the surf breaks. Each morning I would be woken by the sun rising over the ocean, and if the surf looked good, I would paddle straight out and watch the day dawn while waiting for a wave. Local people were very interested in the woman sleeping on the beach and I met lots of residents, both foreigners and Mexicans. Once they realised I didn't have my own, plenty of people offered the use of their showers, toilets, and surf boards.

After several days the place really started to grow on me, mostly due to the surfing, but also due to the friendly people, great vibe and endless desert. There were howling coyotes at night, miles and miles of empty beach, and a slow pace of life. I felt I had found a place to call home for a little, or a long, while.

Over margaritas one evening, a barman said to me: "You're really a rugged kinda gal, aren't you? Goddamn it, you're tough. Hell, you've been sleeping on the beach for two weeks!"

People are actually more likely to call me a surf junky than a rugged kinda gal. That's a label I can't argue with as I've rapidly fallen under the spell of surfing and freely admit my addiction. I can't get enough, I sulk when there are no waves and plan my days around the surf. Life is pretty good. In fact, I think it's fantastic.

Robin Verwest

Robin dismantled her busy life in London, England, during her mid-forties in the aftermath of the 2008 economic crisis and set out to visit two places that had always intrigued her: Alaska, USA, and Baja, Mexico. She pledged to herself that this trip would be longer than the last one (two and a half years) and that she would try surfing. She has just celebrated seven years on the road, has been a surfer for six of them, has visited Alaska and spent a great deal of time in Baja. Robin dedicates her story to a dear friend, Rebecca O'Connell, a strong and beautiful woman who passed away after a fight against breast cancer. This sad loss inspires Robin to continue creating a life filled with love and ingenuity, to live fearlessly, and to follow her heart. She is living her dream and her desire is to see all women do the same.

Evening in the Wrong Barrio

Emily Paskevics

I meant to be inside by sunset. They warned me about
you.
I can't speak your language, which is beautiful but
comes out hard
and sharp from your lips – your tongue barbed,
notched
and fletched. The small fire from your cigarette tip
sparked your eyes for the instant that I scattered
past you – anxious and foreign, collar hitched high,
hair pulled back.

I watched the brutal tattoo
on your neck as you eyed my thighs
or my purse. You muttered something, spat
and struck a laugh, keen to the smell of my fear
like a predator that has already feasted, briefly
disinterested in more meat. I'd go down too
easy, without a sound.

Maybe I reminded you
of the women you have loved in your
uncompromising way, or have just taken –

hissing obscenities, forcing them wide
at those times that you were blood-hungry.

Cleaving sense into me, you thrust a dirty knife
into my notion that this city could somehow
also be mine, when it is yours
and has always been yours
although it offers you nothing
but what you take as your own.

We play survival,
this vicious game which isn't a game,
and for which I have no instincts. Night and day
you stake your territorial claims in this hell
with its crooks, martyrs and hypocrites.

I know nothing of the Hell that you command. I know
nothing of your God, your angry errant God, the God
you erase
nightly and then burn back into life,
lighting candles from cigarettes,
weeping, your God weeping too, the sky and the city
weeping
all over you as you walk alone with a weapon
fisted up in your pocket.

There's more damage
to be done. Face covered to the red rims
of your eyes with a lace kerchief
that could be your mother's,

you glance up and see a woman's face, which is my
face,
this time hiding in the fluorescence
on the safe side of the black-
barred window.

Emily Paskevics

Emily is a writer and editor currently based in Montreal, Canada. She is the author of *The Night Was Animal, or Methods in the Art of Rogue Taxidermy*, and her work can be read in *Hart House Review*, *Vallum Magazine*, *Acta Victoriana*, and *Rogue Agent*, among others. Through OOMPH Press, Emily works with contemporary Hispanic poets, mainly from Colombia, whose work has not yet been translated into English. Read more at www.creativetroublemaking.org and follow her on Twitter: @epaskev.

The Painter of Bluefields

Anna Wrochna

I have been waiting for two hours for the *panga*, a small boat, to arrive so I can start the long journey on Escondido River through the jungle and mangroves that will eventually take me to a Nicaraguan ocean town. Hot and humid, we are all sweating, crushed together against big mammas with small kids on their laps, old grandfathers, chickens tied together by their feet, and huge brown bags full of potatoes, rice, toys and clothes. A real chicken boat, the water transportation version of a chicken bus.

"The *gringa* pays double," I hear a man shouting to the younger guy collecting the trip fee, while he pulls the cord of the motor to finally set off. After fifteen years of travelling and living in these regions (and, for the record, coming from Eastern Europe and not being a real gringa), my head gets a few degrees hotter. I probably should be used to so-called positive discrimination by now. Let's face it, I do come from a more developed and richer region; just the fact I am here means I managed to pay the travel costs of an international trip. But still, I can't stand any kind of discrimination. So I fight back.

"No, *señor*, it's half that price," I say, giving him the exact amount. Then I look away, to the bay full of people selling everything available in the village: sugar cane sweets, mangoes with salt and lemon, water, coconut desserts, small bananas, churros.

I have travelled through sixty countries, lived on four

continents, and I know Latin America more or less from top to bottom. I still have some countries left to visit, but I have managed to explore most of them thoroughly and profoundly.

I feel at home in Latin America. As a matter of fact, I believe I was a Latina in my previous life. It just feels right for me to be here. I am comfortable here and I felt this way even before I had two half-Latina daughters. It is not just the openness and warmth of the people, the varied and interesting cultures, tasty food, pleasant climate, historic places, and natural beauty. It is also the ease I feel when I travel, how I connect to each place, village and community. The support other mothers, grandmothers and fathers have given me when I'm with my kids, being able to talk to anyone on the street without being judged, making friends anywhere with anyone. I never feel alone or in danger, there is always someone to help me out.

Thinking back to my trips alone in this region, I have had the experiences of my life. I fell deeply in love in a cactus desert in Mexico, watching the stars of other far-away galaxies while listening to the UFO stories told by local men. I have visited volcanoes with hot thermals, survived natural disasters and conflicts, and witnessed peace processes. I have met shamans who performed purifying rituals and walked over snowy peaks and through steamy jungles and gazed at desert pyramids.

As I think about those experiences, the boat travels rapidly through the water. The sun is setting and it starts to rain. Small, soft drops at first and then a downpour. No worries; rain in this region comes every afternoon. The boat man hands out a huge piece of black plastic for us passengers to hold above our heads and we look at each other in the dark, humid space as if we were kids playing hide and seek. I think back and remember why I decided to take this trip.

This journey is special. It's a trip into the past. I have managed to get away from my kids for a few days. That's an amazing delight after six years of taking flights, buses and boats with tired, fidgeting, talking, laughing and crying babies and toddlers while carrying buggies and huge bags of toys, food, and everything needed for rain, sun, cold, sickness and emergencies. I feel like the individual I was before I became a mum, a colleague and a housewife.

I am excited about this trip. I am going to interview a talented local painter in a magical city. After a decade, I'm going to meet him again. I see myself ten years ago, setting off on this same trip. I was young and adventurous, I felt lucky to be sent on an election observation mission to Bluefields, Nicaragua. The name in itself was so intriguing. A coastal town with an English name, cut off from the majority of the country, where even in the twenty-first century you can only arrive by boat or plane. I imagined the first pirate, Abraham Blauvelt, who gave his name to the town, arriving at this far-away bay trying to find his fortune. He wasn't the only one. Bluefields was a hiding place for English and Dutch buccaneers in the seventeenth century, and it was the capital of the English protectorate over the funnily named Mosquito Coast. An important Caribbean port, it's home to a diverse mix of people.

Finally, we get off the boat. We all try to stretch our legs. I ignore the young man trying to convince me to stay in what he considers to be the best hotel in town. I just want to walk in the old park, in the colourful market, along the shore with its wooden houses standing on sticks to fight the floods, all the way to the main historic street.

Ten years ago I walked on the same street with a local girl who was showing me the city. We stopped at a pharmacy to buy some pills. As I entered, I looked around and saw dozens of colourful paintings on the wall. I asked the pharmacist who had painted all those colours and she offered to introduce me to the painter. Sure, why not? It could be an interesting discussion with an old man who had spent his life in Bluefields painting. When I stopped by in the afternoon, I was surprised to see a young, handsome guy coming out of his studio. Long, brown curly hair, a beard, and a big smile. He was no doubt interested in this international attention and we set up an evening meeting at a bar.

On those hot nights in the Caribbean, the streets turned into a big party. Salsa bars in old colonial buildings, loud Latin music, dancing on the streets in the dark, the best Cuba Libres to forget the daily struggle. I could see the freedom on the faces of the old men who asked the young tourists to dance to the never ending bachata songs, and everyone seemed like one big family.

I met the young painter, who lived in one of the old yellow houses on the main street, and we watched the colourful crowd from one of those centuries-old balconies that have seen civil wars, marches, funerals, and weddings. We talked about history, culture, life experiences, hobbies, and travels. Even though we were from different cultures, we made an instant connection. Inside the half-lit room full of antiques, with the sounds of music from the street, we sat on an old sofa and kissed. My memories from that night are blurred, but I remember the lights, the music, the fan and the sofa.

The next morning I had to leave for Managua to finish my mission, but at the last moment, we had a crazy idea. Let's meet in Ometepe, the famous volcano island in the middle of Lake Nicaragua, in five days. He planned the trip, a bold move that was based on faith and good luck in an age before mobile phones.

I arrived a day early and saw the need for the God of Fortune to bring us lovers together, as we had no set place or time to meet. Miraculously, when I had almost given up and lost faith after searching and waiting for hours, he appeared in the middle of the street. We spent a romantic day in this little end-of-the-world place, slept in hammocks, watched the sunset, ate fish, and enjoyed the warm climate and the coolness of the mountain.

But that day ended and I had to catch my flight back to

Europe. I went to Managua while he flew back to Bluefields. I was surprised when on my last day, he appeared in front of my hotel in the capital city with his big smile. He showed me around Managua, invited me to a small house and painting studio he had in the suburbs there, and showed me how committed and emotional a Latin lover can be.

He accompanied me to the airport and there he gave me a long hug. There was something strange in his eyes, it was like he was saying: "Let's see if life will allow us to meet again." He rolled up a canvas painting and tied it to my bag. He had painted a portrait of me, which I would save for the next ten years.

A very sad goodbye.

I remember all this while watching the ocean coast of Bluefields. I now feel ready to face him again. With a headache from the long, hot trip, I set off to find a pharmacy. I enter the closest one, look up, and see those colourful paintings. They smile down on me, the way they did a decade ago.

Anna Wrochna

Anna, who is of Hungarian-Polish origins, has travelled to sixty countries and lived and worked in twelve countries on four continents, but Latin America is still the place where she feels most at home. She studied in Mexico, observed elections in Ecuador and Nicaragua, travelled through Cuba and Guatemala, worked on development projects in Ethiopia, India, Pakistan and El Salvador, and helped develop regional women's rights campaigns in Bangladesh. Anna currently lives in Colombia where she works for a human rights organisation and travels with her young daughters.

Witness to the Crime

Jade Griffiths

While travelling in Guatemala, I posted a status on social media about having been attacked, along with photos of my swollen and bruised face, and many wrongly assumed that a local person had attacked me.

Even though I pointed out that the British man I was travelling with, my boyfriend at the time (we'll call him Carl), had assaulted me, many still found a way to blame the country I was in. My sister told me that Guatemala was a country that did not respond well to domestic abuse and nothing would be done. Friends urged me to come home, immediately, as I was obviously not safe 'out there.'

This could not have been further from the truth. Yes, I had been attacked. Yes, it was in Guatemala. No, it was not the fault of the country or its people.

I will not go into too much detail about that night, except to say that the attack happened around midnight, in the fairly isolated house where we were staying. To escape I had to run down almost a hundred earth and log steps, then along a long lane and up a very steep hill, aiming for the main road.

I came across two local men on a bicycle. One of them knew me, and he sat with me while the other man cycled to the police station. I was trembling with fear and my whole body and face were in pain. Carl had followed me and reached the top of the hill at the moment the police arrived. He was shouting and aggressive and the police guessed it was him. After checking, they handcuffed Carl and put him in the back seat of the police pickup truck with some officers. I was placed in the truck bed along with the local men and their bicycle.

After dropping Carl at the police station, the officers took me to a health centre and asked a doctor to check me over. I was still in a state of shock and when the doctor said he was going to give me an injection, I started to scream. "I don't want to go to sleep," I cried. "I don't want him to come and get me."

The policemen calmed me down and assured me that Carl would not be let out that night. The doctor reassured me that the injection would not make me drowsy, it would just relieve the pain and reduce some of the swelling in my face.

Afterwards, the officers took me back to the station for questioning. They asked me to go through what had happened and they were very patient. They asked me where I would like to be taken and I opted for a friend's house. I couldn't sleep that night, so I stayed up with my friend and made my way back to my house as soon as the sun rose. Later that morning, the Ministerio Publico (Guatemala's body of independent public prosecutors) called and came to collect me. They took me by boat to the mainland where I made an official statement and was medically checked, complete with photographs. I was offered a translator but I declined because I am proficient in Spanish. I was surprised by the efficiency, promptness, and understanding shown by every individual in that agency.

I feel that domestic abuse is taken very seriously in Guatemala. The case was taken to court and Carl was not granted bail. I was provided with a psychologist for support and a translator. Although questioned, I was never doubted nor made to feel like any of this had been my fault.

The psychological implications of this cannot be explained briefly. I was in a state of shock, I felt vulnerable and weak, and I was battling with the complex emotions involved in a domestic attack. Carl had been detained immediately and the whole process had been undertaken with minimal involvement from my side, which meant I could concentrate on healing, both emotionally and physically. The fact that Carl was charged, whether I wanted him to be or not, meant there could be no pressure from him or from his family to withdraw the charges.

I was, in effect, a witness to the crime.

Local people were extremely supportive. My Mayan and Garifuna neighbours rallied round with natural tinctures, teas and various remedies designed to bring down the swelling on my face and make me stronger. If it had not been for one local friend, I would not have eaten at all in the week that followed the attack, because I had lost my appetite. I passed that friend's house every day, as I took my walk along the beach, and every time he asked me if I had eaten. When I shook my head, he gave me the plate of food he had saved for me and I slowly picked through it.

I still marvel at how smoothly this attack was dealt with by the Guatemalan authorities and the way this community provided the kindness and the support I needed to get through it. I am forever in debt to this country, and its people, and that is why I return to it, time and time again.

Jade Griffiths

Jade is a psychology graduate from Wales who plans to open a healing retreat in Guatemala. She is a single parent and home educates her eleven-year-old daughter, Jahzara. She has travelled both alone and with Jahzara in China, Australia, the USA, Europe, and Central America and dreams about the pair making a mother-and-daughter trip across South America in a van. Jade is a self-confessed hippie whose hobbies include aerial silks and playing the guitar. She loves festivals and reggae music.

The Swim

Caitlin Furio

The first time I read the description in my guidebook, I slammed the book shut, shivered and thought, "How did they know?"

Northern Nicaragua had appealed to me for its cool mountain weather, political culture, diverse ecosystems, spectacular hiking and world-class coffee. After three weeks in the region I was full of caffeine, politics and mountain air, but I was missing the one experience I had craved the most: hiking in a cloud forest.

Much of the Central American cloud forest has been developed into farmland, and opportunities to experience it are surprisingly difficult to find. As a result, I'd become obsessed with reaching one particular location, a remote mountain village called Peñas Blancas. The guidebook's description of the village was: "Here you'll find the mossy, misty, life-altering primary cloud forest scenery you've been waiting for."

Weeks after reading that sentence, I realized I had just one spare day in my schedule. The life-altering cloud forests of Peñas Blancas were a three-hour bus ride in the opposite direction. It was a fool's journey to go there for one night, but I was determined to make it happen.

I asked the owner of the hostel where I was staying for some advice. He told me about a man called Don Chico who had spent every one of his seventy-eight years exploring the cliffs of Peñas Blancas. Don Chico ran a small eco-tourism business in the village, led guided hikes through the cloud forest, and rented out his extra bedroom to visitors. The hostel owner assured me that the few travelers he knew who had visited Peñas Blancas had all returned with rave reviews of Don Chico.

I awoke early the next morning and caught a chicken bus into the mountains. Chicken buses are those old U.S. school buses that have been given a new lease of life by Central America's persistent mechanics and relaxed safety laws. The buses are patched-up, repainted in audacious colors, fitted with booming sound systems and driven over anything that resembles a road. A good chicken bus ride is both cheap transportation and an entertaining experience. A bad chicken bus ride is a nightmare.

My journey to Peñas Blancas was the latter. Human bodies, bags of produce, baskets of tortillas, plastic furniture and a random assortment of other items filled every inch of space. I felt claustrophobic as the run-down bus creaked into the mountains and was relieved when the half-seat at the back of the bus became vacant. It was only big enough for one person and I assumed it would give me some breathing room.

That was my mistake.

I had been very apprehensive about traveling Latin America. I don't speak Spanish and I can't dance, which seemed like good enough reasons to prioritize the thousands of other places I wanted to visit. My trip had happened almost by accident. I had volunteered in Belize and the opportunity to travel Central America after I finished was too good to miss. Even so, I was nervous about being a woman traveling alone. I had traveled a lot before, but rarely alone.

Most of the people I had met in Nicaragua had been helpful and welcoming. I had experienced very little outright harassment. I had not even been catcalled, because Nicaraguan men tend to make a strange hissing noise under their breath instead. Although it's unnerving, it's easier to ignore than the jeers I've received in other countries.

The vendors on the bus to Peñas Blancas were determined to deliver every bit of harassment I had thus far avoided. They climbed onto the bus, shouted that they had *plantanitos* or *gaseosas* for sale and stood by the back door so they could hiss and stare at me while they waited for the next stop.

"*Plantanitos, mami?*" they asked me and, "Do you have a boyfriend?" Sometimes they employed the little English they knew and leered at me: "Hello, baby." A group soon gathered to watch my discomfort. The more I ignored them, the more they laughed.

I went to college in Boston, a city widely considered one of the safest in the United States. One weekend during my second year, I visited a friend across town for a late dinner and movie and rode home alone on the last subway train of the night. The train car was almost empty so I took a single seat for myself.

Shortly before the train departed, one more person stumbled into the car. He was tall, white, shaggy-haired and obviously tipsy. He took the seat behind me.

I could tell he was feeling chatty, so I pulled a book out of my bag.

He ignored the hint.

"Hi," he said. I sighed and looked up, which was enough to encourage him. He chatted incessantly for half an hour. He described his night and gave me a long list of his favorite bars in Boston. It was annoying, but it seemed innocent enough.

We were within a few stops of my destination when I prepared to stand up and leave. The sight of this caused an abrupt change in his attitude.

"You're into weird sex, aren't you?" he said. "Wait a few more stops and get off with me. You're into the weird stuff, I can tell. Let me eat you out."

I stared at him, appalled. What had happened to the drunk, rambling idiot I had been ignoring a few moments before? He flicked his tongue at me and grinned.

My stomach lurched. He had suddenly become threatening. I felt angry at myself for letting the conversation reach this point. Why had I even acknowledged him?

I took my first opportunity to escape and jumped off the train at the next stop, which was one station before mine. He shouted, "Come on, you know you want it," as I sprinted around the corner.

My heart was beating heavily and I couldn't unclench my fists. I knew I was too rattled to return to my empty apartment so I hurried to a friend's house nearby. When I arrived, I found a group gathered around a board game. One girl looked at me with sympathy and handed me a beer.

"That, my dear," she said. "Is why you never take the last train of the night."

By the time the bus lurched to a halt in Peñas Blancas, I was feeling anxious about my plans with the mysterious Don Chico. Why had I jumped on a bus to meet a random man in a random place in a foreign country? How would I contact him if I couldn't find him? Did I even have a backup option if lodging with him fell through?

He was waiting for me when I arrived, an elderly man wearing waist high jeans, a baseball cap and rubber boots. He broke into a wrinkled grin when he saw me and I could see his gold-rimmed teeth shining beneath his Charlie Chaplin mustache.

Don Chico walked with me to his house, chatting the whole time. I relaxed as I recognized the characteristic Nicaraguan hospitality and kindness in his demeanor. He spoke Spanish in a lilting mumble that was friendly but almost impossible to understand. I locked onto the key parts of every sentence and let the rest fall away, hoping it wouldn't matter.

He showed me to my room. It was a simple concrete, tin-roofed affair with multiple fleece blankets to protect against the cold mountain nights. He gave me an excellent cup of coffee and my own pair of rubber boots and we began to hike.

We turned one corner and there they were: the white cliffs of Peñas Blancas. They peaked above our heads, glistening and ghostly amongst the morning clouds. The bleached stones were draped in cloud forest, a rich tangle of giant cathedral trees, bromeliads and orchids that echoed with birdsong.

"*Lista?*" Don Chico asked, grinning at my awed expression. "Are you ready?"

The steep hike up to the cliffs took an hour and a half. There were moments when we gained nearly vertical altitude, climbing worn wooden ladders or using the tree roots to hoist ourselves up. We crept along narrow, muddy trails that overlooked steep declines, gorgeous old-growth trees, and the rolling hills of Nicaragua.

Don Chico bounced ahead of me, beaming and chattering and providing specific instructions as to how to handle the trickiest parts.

"Put this foot here and that foot there," he would say and, "Grab this tree... no, not that one!" He laughed the entire time with light, childish giggles.

He was a hilarious hiking partner. His whole demeanor was giddy with enthusiasm, whether he was explaining the medicinal use of a plant or swinging from a vine. He was also intent on me taking thousands of pictures. At one point, he stopped mid-step and looked down. He pulled a rock from the ground beside the trail and placed it between two tree roots in front of him.

"It looks like a dancing man!" he laughed. "Take a picture."

Another time he stopped to point out one of the elephantine leaves that dotted the undergrowth. The plant drooped onto the trail, its leaves as tall as Don Chico. I began to take a picture but he stopped me.

"No, no," he said, "Like this." He moved behind the leaf and put his head in the crevice so the enormous leaf covered his whole body. I laughed and took the picture.

The higher we climbed, the more frequently I stopped to

stare at the forest. The trees rose in towers around us, dozens of feet wide and dripping with air plants and orchids. Vines and plants of every variety fell from the branches to the ground, creating a curtain of plant life between us and the valleys below. The white cliffs peeked out from beside us and glittered in the sunlight.

As we approached the top, Don Chico pointed at the morning sun, which was blasting through a gap in the canopy. The light clearly belonged to a sunny day yet somehow, in that tiny space in front of the cliff, it looked like it was raining.

Don Chico explained, as far as I believe I understood him, that the water was condensation from the forest's namesake clouds. It dripped from the roots and leaves of the plants above us. The sun blazed through the droplets and gave the trees and cliffs an ethereal glow. Standing there, haunted by the sound of invisible birds and gazing into that incredible light, was one of the most magical moments of my life.

Don Chico and I pushed onwards until we reached the top of the cliff and the forest stretched out below us. We were surrounded by mammoth trees, mossy branches and dazzling butterflies.

His zealous energy became infectious. We bounced forward into the forest and it seemed as if we discovered a new swimming hole or waterfall at every turn. I must have seen fifteen waterfalls over the course of an hour. We stopped to drink the spring water, pouring it into our mouths from huge tropical leaves.

I've always been a water baby. My parents had to drag me out of pools when I was very young. I used to sit chest deep in the ocean and let the waves wash over me until my bathing suit was heavy with sand and my fingers were a study in wrinkles.

In some ways, I aged out of this. Swimming as a teenager became more about the opportunity to preen than playing in the water. The glamour of being a wind-blown beach babe does not correspond to having your hair weighed down by sand, nor wearing a bathing suit sturdy enough to stand up to the waves. The ordeal of being in a bathing suit in a public place soon stopped being a fun chance to swim and simply became stressful and unappealing.

Now, however, I began to feel an emotional distress rising in my chest as we passed each new pool and waterfall. I recognized that feeling immediately. I wanted to swim.

Here I was, at the peak of these ancient cliffs in untouched cloud forest, stumbling across these fantastic swimming holes. Each one teased me more than the last. The water was clear and crisp and speckled with the sunlight that streamed through the leaves above. The pools were like images from a dream, nature at its most idyllic. My heart ached with the desire to jump in.

How could I? I had several hours of hiking left with Don Chico, and I couldn't hike in wet clothes. I would have to swim in my bra and underwear in front of Don Chico. The thought horrified me.

I'm not sure whether Don Chico realized what I was thinking or whether the fates were conspiring against me, but at the next pool he asked if I wanted to swim. I looked at him and stalled. I couldn't speak Spanish well enough to express my doubts or ask him exactly what he meant. I was all alone in my decision.

I thought about how this seemed like exactly the sort of common sense situation travel books and my mother would tell me to avoid. I thought about my underwear. I thought about all those men on the bus in Nicaragua, and the man on the train in Boston, and men in general. I thought about Don Chico's innocent, toothy grin. I thought about how I would feel if I left this perfect swimming hole, with its perfect water, without swimming in it. I thought about the immense amount

of privilege, effort, luck, money and time that had gotten me to the foot of this waterfall, at the top of this cliff, in this remote region of northern Nicaragua. I thought about how unfair it was that I even had to think when a male traveler would already be splashing around in the water. I thought until Don Chico looked at me with some concern.

I thought about the kindness and the welcome that Don Chico and most Nicaraguans had shown me throughout my trip. I thought about rising above the intimidation of being a solo female traveler and taking ahold of the moment. I thought for one more second, stripped down to my bra and underwear, and dove into the water.

It was the best swim of my life.

Caitlin Furio

Caitlin is a writer, map-maker, budget traveler, musician, idealist, and vegetable enthusiast. After a few years struggling to feel satisfied by the standard U.S. career track, she quit her office job in Philadelphia to volunteer with a conservation organization in Belize. She went on to travel Central America for 101 days, visiting Nicaragua, El Salvador, Guatemala, Mexico, and Cuba. While abroad, Caitlin began writing blog posts to keep her friends and family updated on her adventures. Her website soon evolved into *Furiosities*, a travel blog documenting the beauty, humor and inspiration she has discovered in the world through travel. Read more about Caitlin and her travels at www.furiosities.com.

The Legacy of Berta Cáceres

Gloria Jiménez

It was getting dark. We were in Utopia, a community center in a remote farming community, and the departure of the sunlight put a natural end to the day's activities. Our group was undeterred by the darkness, which seemed all the more omnipotent as we looked out onto the grazing land surrounding the compound. The few neighboring houses had willingly surrendered to the night and were consumed by it; if not for the mooing of the cattle, you wouldn't even know they were there.

We sat at the communal tables in the courtyard chatting, encouraged by the candlelight that gave us only glimpses of each other's faces. I had been staring at the pot on the traditional cooking stove for an hour, watching the embers of the firewood glow as the pot's lid danced and liquid sputtered out. No food had been served and I suspected there was not enough for everyone. Resigned to skipping dinner, I sipped my coffee and felt warmed by it on such a cool night. I was exhausted but awaiting the arrival of Berta Cáceres, leader of the Civic Council of Popular and Indigenous Organizations of Honduras (COPINH).

By the time I met Berta in the late summer of 2016, she was already a force inside and outside Honduras. She had famously hidden in the mountains on the border with Nicaragua during the 2009 coup with others in the opposition movement who were also being persecuted. She had built an organization for the preservation and advancement of Indigenous Lenca. Not just an organization, she had built a movement that was transcending borders and threatening the status quo. Her enemies were the powers-that-be, the Honduran state, multinational companies and those who perpetuated a wave of privatization over those at the bottom.

I barely knew Berta, much less what she represented, but when she strolled in and flashed her bright smile, I buckled under her greatness and struggled to introduce myself. It was late and after a brief exchange, the evening was over. We were escorted to our quarters, a large room with ten bunk beds.

It was one of my first trips to Honduras and I was confronting the types of violence that rarely make the headlines in the United States, political violence that implicated the Honduran state with foreign powers as accomplices. My mind raced as I lay in bed. I thought about Berta's enemies. Her profile was ascending and her support kept growing. They wanted to silence her. The louder she yelled, and the more voices joined hers, the more they wanted her dead. It was silent in the room, apart from the occasional mutter and creak of a bed. I lay on the bottom bunk under a thick wool blanket, wrapped like a mummy. My body was tense, as if staying still could somehow keep the cold and fear away. We were on a remote compound a good distance from the center of town and any witnesses. I saw in my mind's eye the flimsy, barely six-foot fence and wondered what protection it could offer. I thought about the double doors of the compound. Would they hold back intruders? Nothing more than a wooden log barricaded the doors. Nor was I reassured by the police post at the main entrance of the community. It was the same police who came in tanks and hurled tear gas at those who demanded justice in Honduras, and in some cases they did much worse.

As my paranoia snowballed it would have helped to have remembered my mother's awed chastisements in response to the things I was doing or about to do. Such as my decision to sleep within reach of that brave and hunted soul named Berta Cáceres.

I was in a place where violence is not random; it is targeted at those who challenge and hope to dismantle the oppressive system in power. Of course, not all of Honduras is dangerous. The elite hide behind gated communities and people in rural areas often lead more peaceful lives. There are those in the middle and lower classes who do not consider themselves political, who just want to get by and avoid being victims of violence, and there are those in the opposition movement who know they risk their lives by speaking out. It is hard to deny that the Honduran people are being crushed under the heel of a dictatorship and unfettered capitalism. Berta was one of the few nationally and internationally recognized opposition leaders in Honduras who was organizing and empowering people to stand up and resist and return to their roots of collectivism, the antithesis of capitalism.

Berta was assassinated a few months after we met, a brutal event that sent shock waves across Honduras and the world. Within weeks of her death, I witnessed the forced displacement of an indigenous community who had been battling to reclaim their land. They were the rightful owners of a communal land title but their land had been illegally privatized and sold. The community was part of COPINH, the organization Berta had led. When it was over, we discovered that a second COPINH member, Nelson García, had been assassinated. He had been with us just hours before his death.

The community had started a land recuperation process two years earlier but when I met them they were being forced out. Dozens of families had held on, living in makeshift shacks and hoping that justice would prevail. An outsider looking at this now militarized site could have only concluded that that they were watching an anti-gang operation, when in fact these people were peaceful, highly vulnerable members of Honduras' society who had dared to fight for their rights.

I watched one child, barefoot and crying, follow his mother who carried a trash bag filled with their belongings to an empty plot of land. Another woman spoke to us with a tone of defiance and conviction. "*¿Quién dijo miedo?*" she said. "Who's afraid?" She was shouting, not looking at the police officer who escorted us, but clearly addressing him. "Like Berta said, I'm a woman who has her ovaries in the right place. We will be back. This won't end here."

Berta deconstructed and reconstructed what it meant to be a woman. She challenged women to break free from the repressive social constructs of what constituted acceptable behavior for a woman, particularly in the context of social and political change. As a leader making change, she illustrated not only the possibility but the necessity of women being the protagonists when it comes to ending societal ills such as racism, capitalism and sexism. That part of her legacy will never be erased.

I tried not to intervene but it felt meaningless to follow standard protocols in the face of such a raw human experience. I slipped away from my police escort and wandered between the houses. I helped people take apart their homes, not just the physical structures but the dreams and aspirations, and the realization of the basic human rights of safety and well-being that lay within those four walls. I took a hammer, focusing my disgust at the situation with every swing. That evicted family comprised of a grandmother, a mother, a toddler and a litter of kittens that kept hiding in the discarded boards. Every now and again we had to stop what we were doing to prevent the kittens from being crushed.

I felt like I witnessed humanity at its worst that day, but somehow the community remained resilient. Some worked quietly but others laughed and chatted as they made trips back and forth. These families had done something remarkable. They had stood up to injustice and actively rejected the state's abuse of power. They may have lost their battle, but they had widened the crack in a system that will one day, hopefully, collapse.

It was a hot and humid day, and a dizzying one. A judge read some sort of statement regarding the eviction and that led to a shouting match between the judge and those being evicted and the supposed holder of the land's title. The tension increased when news filtered through about Nelson García's assassination. It seemed only fitting that as we tried to leave, our engine wouldn't start. I was sweaty and drained as we pushed the truck away.

You can never really escape. When one of our brothers or sisters suffers, humanity suffers too. Liberation is interdependent. I knew that as soon our truck was fixed we would leave, but I knew that the world would still be broken.

Gloria Jiménez

Gloria is a Mexican/Salvadoran writer, activist, and aspiring software developer from Los Angeles, USA. She has lived in many countries in both Latin America and Asia, accompanying communities in resistance. Gloria has seen the good, the bad, and the ugly of the non-profit world and would rather be an unpaid soldier of liberation. Gloria's idea of a dream vacation is being at a cat café in Tokyo, Japan, with a fluffy cat on her lap and a latte in her hand. Connect with Gloria on LinkedIn (www.linkedin.com/in/gloriajimenez).

Gift of Grapes

Kate Rawles

I'm on a long, straight stretch of road in the desert in Northern Peru. I've been cycling for five hours in a strange new world, through landscapes I can't read. It's like riding through an immense quarry, with miles and miles of sand-coloured chiselled flats and slopes. I can't tell which bits are natural, and which have actually been quarried.

Over every dry river bed there are clouds of swallows dancing in the air like oversized gnats. The newness is exciting. And the straightness is challenging; the kind of road where a sign announcing a bend is a major event. Hardened to traffic after four months on the Pan-American Highway, now there is none. It's just me, the swallows and an occasional hawk.

Out of the heat a grey car emerges and passes me from behind. It slows, pulls over and stops. Engine churning the air. Bollocks. No other vehicles, no buildings. I can't out-pedal any car, let alone this sleek machine. The window slides down. Single man inside. His arm emerges, creased blue shirt sleeve. Waves me down. I stop. What else can I do?

"Where are you from?" he asks from behind dark glasses, as time goes just a little bit crinkly.

"England," I say.

"I'm from Colombia," he says. "Please, take these bananas and a mandarin orange...."

Back in 1992 a girlfriend and I decided to cycle from Caracas, Venezuela, through Colombia to Guayaquil in Ecuador. Everyone told us we were crazy and would surely die.

Two young women, cycling man-less in South America? And through Colombia? The sole exception to these dire warnings came from Hilary Bradt, the travel writer and guidebook author, and probably the only person we spoke to who had actually been to South America.

"You will have a fabulous time," she said. "Especially in Colombia."

She was right. Of the many things I learned on that trip, the most vivid was to pay most attention to people who have been where you are going, ideally in the way you are going there.

Now, twenty-five years later, I'm back in South America. I've quit my job and am taking a year to cycle from Cartagena to Cape Horn (well, that's the ambition, anyway) on a bamboo bike that I built myself. My aim is to use the journey to explore and champion biodiversity and why it matters. Among other things, this is turning out to be a sure-fire way to meet all sorts of inspiring, committed, interesting people working in South American nature conservation. And this time, I have the huge advantage of setting out knowing that Colombia, at least, is bursting with kind and friendly people and that, however turbulent and however much violence is still in its seams, as a traveller this kindness is overwhelmingly what I'll encounter. I'm assuming this will almost certainly be true of the other countries on my route, too.

However, I haven't been on the road for any length of time in ten years. What little Spanish I used to speak has evaporated. I am rusty, and I am on my own. Looking back at my departure from Cartagena, up and over many roads, I can still feel the sense of inner-eyes-out-on-stalks as I took that first pedal push. Maybe it will always be like this when I make that initial move into a space that feels so daunting. Whatever lies ahead I don't yet know whether I can deal with it, or how I will deal with it. Everything changes when I make the first move.

Santa Marta is not on the way from Cartagena to Cape Horn. It's about one hundred and fifty miles up the coast to the north east. But, with a bunch of invites to visit various conservation projects in that direction, it seemed at the time like a minor and worthy detour. So, finally, after various false starts, Woody the bamboo bike and I launched ourselves into the Cartagena traffic and headed up the coast.

I had been a tad concerned about the taxis, which flock the city in yellow hooting multitudes. The taxis were just fine. Other vehicles, though, were another matter. The buses were demonic. They are all in some rival warfare with each other, and they blast past, multi-coloured and blaring, cutting corners and focused on outmanoeuvring other buses rather than staying on the road. I inched out into the traffic, stopped at the slightest doubt, raced around parked objects, and pushed across every busy junction. It was hair-raising. And you can't focus solely on the buses because the road is filled with potholes, motorcycles constantly switching in all directions, people pushing carts, and sudden piles of gravel. Out on the road along the coast things calmed down slightly, but only slightly. A huge wind was blowing – against me, of course with sand and grit.

The first lesson I learned was about headwinds. These were a Good Thing, at least in that I was heading north but would mostly be heading south, and that they swirled up the heat with a genuine sliver of sea breeze, fractionally reducing the oven effect. But they were at times so strong I had to get off and cling to the bike to stay upright. They also slowed me down. A lot. End result, loss of daylight.

My second lesson was about cycling in the dark. A wonderful thing in many circumstances, but not as an introduction to the city of Barranquilla. Having congratulated myself the night before for somehow finding the only hostel/hotel in Galerazamba or indeed anywhere on my route so far, I assumed that finding a place in large and populous Barranquilla would be a breeze. I ended up slogging uphill on an endless main street with a battering headwind in fading light in horrible traffic and then weaving about looking for cheap hotels that appeared on maps.me but not on the ground.

By the time the third one failed to materialise, it was dark and the traffic was still bonkers even at nine o'clock at night. Then I bumped into a Park Inn, complete with liveried doorman. Deciding my life was at stake, I tentatively enquired about the price of a room. It was about US$60 rather than the many thousands I'd imagined. And so, wielding an emergency credit card and with my frugality temporarily on hold, I was suddenly in safe air-conditioned luxury and had the best shower ever (and the only hot one in Colombia so far.) Woody was, of course, safely installed with me in my twelfth floor room.

I learned lesson three, exit strategies, the next day. Having studied an online map, I came up with a super smart plan to outwit the traffic by taking a minor road out of Barranquilla that ran close to the sea. I harboured fantasies of a really nice lunch once I had survived the town centre traffic and was on the coast road heading out of town. The road became quieter, but the lunch fantasy receded as I found myself cycling through an industrial site covered in razor-wire on one side and sludgy water and acres of grim-looking shanty towns on the other.

I was soon flagged down by a woman on a scooter, who, realising my goal – getting across the bridge towards Santa Marta – shook her head in horror and said *muchos rateros*. The translation is pickpockets but her sign language suggested something a tad more unpleasant. In deciding to escape the traffic it hadn't occurred to me that I might be venturing into risks of another type. The stereotype of dangerous Colombia had long ago been replaced in my head by experiences with helpful and welcoming Colombia.

My scooter guardian insisted on escorting me to the Santa Marta road bridge, stopping at all checkpoints to inform them of the stupid gringa on a bicycle with obviously expensive panniers full of presumably valuable stuff. Finally, we reached the junction where she pulled up at a parked police van and explained the situation. The policeman grinned, shook his head and then my hand, and then waved me onto the bridge, the wrong way up a one-way slip road and into a gap in the traffic.

I visited some truly brilliant nature conservation projects, including schools whose entire curriculum is designed around turtles and a project to protect the habitat of highly endangered and endemic Cotton Top Monkeys. As I cycled back towards Cartagena, lesson four, never feel smug, became clear. Having congratulated myself on learning lessons one to three, I'd reduced my mileage, done everything I could to ensure I wouldn't be on the road in the dark, and booked somewhere to stay in advance. But the place I'd booked turned out not to exist (or not where Google and maps.me said it did) and I ended up racing through a remote section, trying to out-pedal the swiftly sinking sun, thirty miles to go to the next possible stop with not quite enough time or water.

Hot, dry-mouthed and working hard, I stopped to harness the magical power of music. Pulling away again into the heat with Cheryl Crow blasting "I'm not the kind of girl you take home," I had a moment of sheer, piercing happiness. Somehow, for all the toughness and challenges, this was absolutely the right place to be.

Four months into the journey, I like to think I'm a bit more streetwise now. And many of the initial less-than-helpful inner (and outer) voices, the ones that say you are too small, too impractical, too afraid, too shy, too blonde, too bad at navigating, too alone to do this have mostly fallen quiet. I am strong enough and practical enough. I don't need to be superwoman to cycle slowly south.

What I mostly need and want now is a way to stay open, to stay connected with the ability to see what's around me with the same vividness I did at the start. And to stay connected with that fabulously energising surge of life lessons that I got in the novelty of the first few weeks.

I've learned to take nothing for granted. The basics are so very precious. Especially here, where not everyone has them. Clean, cold water. Shade. Somewhere safe (however full of crickets) to sleep. Food. Even if, as a vegetarian in a carnivorous culture, food is your third meal of rice and eggs that day. I've long grappled with how simply feeling grateful can liberate you from so much ego-related rubbish and generate such deep, easy happiness. And yet it is such a hard state of mind to sustain in normal life (or the not-really-normal life I've become accustomed to).

I've been reminded, over and over, how travelling alone, perhaps especially as a woman alone, changes your interactions with other people. In a couple or a group, you can be perceived as a closed and self-sufficient unit. Turn up solo, and people take you very differently. You are seen as more open and, perhaps, more vulnerable. Add a bike with heavily loaded panniers – or a large backpack – and you have an out-and-out invitation for people to come and talk. Where are you going? Where have you been? Can't you afford a car? Can we buy you lunch? On your own on a bike or on foot you interact differently with the birds and the sky and the plants and the mountains too.

The protectiveness that a woman travelling alone can trigger here is sometimes exasperating, sometimes moving. Cartagena is now two thousand five hundred miles away and I cycled here all by myself and you are telling me I should stay off the roads because the traffic is dangerous? Or insisting you push the bike across this junction for me? Sometimes I feel safer as a woman in South America, as the chivalry in the culture spills out into a protectiveness towards this lone, strange woman on her strange and laden bike. Sometimes, my sheer existence as a single traveller sparks a defensive reaction in others. They rush to tell me all the reasons why it's dangerous as if, on some level, they are grappling with a need to justify why they wouldn't dream of travelling alone themselves. Or perhaps would dream but not do.

I am fascinated by the astonishing diversity of landscapes and wildlife, from Pacific to Caribbean coastlines, from steppe to high mountains, from the lizards that scoot back from the roadside, to the vultures picking over road kill to the occasional glimpse of coati to the frigate birds hanging in the sky like gigantic swallows. The flavours of new fruits. And, perhaps above all, the human contact and friendliness and generosity. Coconut biscuits and mango juice and a gift of grapes as I leave a roadside food stall.

On a darker note, I am confronted again and again by the fact that, bar terrible bad luck, the dangers that exist in these lands have and will always have vastly more impact on the people that live here than they ever will on travellers. Although at times I've had an unnerving sense of being only just ahead of those dangers, as if the world were closing in behind me.

Mud avalanches in towns I'd just cycled through. A kidnapping in a village I'd just left, very specific, an internal ELN thing, I was told later. Not to worry as a gringa. And there are constant stories of corruption and of what happens when environmentalists and others try to change the status quo; when they rattle up against the boundaries of power and money. Of the obscene, distorted domination of the mining and oil industries on governments and democratic decision making. To really court danger, be a human rights advocate in Colombia, or challenge a mining company's decision to mine for copper or gold in Ecuador, never mind that the mine will pollute your community's water and land for centuries to come. Travelling as a woman alone is nothing compared to any of that.

Even so, the boundaries of "Can I go there?" have not entirely dissolved. They just shift. Relaxed about things that woke me in the night four months ago, a new, troubling unknown emerges. Lately, a new worry is a long stretch of desert road ahead with nothing on it. By nothing and long I mean, no hostels, no shops, no cafés, no houses, and too far

to cycle in one or possibly two days. My tent has so far only been used only as a makeshift room in nature conservation offices, typically with an overnight guard nearby. I am still nervous about camping alone.

But what is the option here? Take a bus? Hitch a ride? And here is where the Latin American magic starts to flicker onto the scene.

I am worrying away at this in my head when a cyclist appears, going the other way. A woman! We stop. Two solo *ciclistas*, delighted to meet one another. There's a fast exchange of hugs and information. Frederika from Sweden has just been where I'm going. It's wonderful, camping in the desert, she says. There's nobody there. So what is there to fear, from nobody?

"You will love it," she says.

I did love it. I saw a desert fox, heard the bird song in the morning. Afterwards, savouring that gift of unexpected reassurance and its timing, I almost can't believe she was real.

Savour all of it. From each challenge learn a bit more about who you are and how you can be; generous, alive and open to the world. Approach the world in good faith and assume the best of everyone, until you have evidence otherwise; and keep your antennae super alert for that evidence, always.

Don't be naively trusting but know that, in the crazy traffic and heat, or on that empty road, or in the rain, or whatever it is that is making you uncertain, you are in Latin America. Soon enough someone will step forward and offer you a bunch of bananas. Or a fresh mango juice. Or a lift. Or a cup of coffee. Or the names of the lizards. Or a big smile. Or a gift of grapes.

And you will be just fine.

Kate Rawles

Kate is passionate about using adventurous journeys to raise awareness and inspire action on our major environmental challenges. A former university lecturer in environmental philosophy, she set up Outdoor Philosophy to explore the big questions about human/nature relations – and how to improve them. She is currently on The Life Cycle journey, traveling from Colombia to Cape Horn by bamboo bike and exploring biodiversity: what it is, why it matters and what can be done to protect it. Previous 'adventure plus' journeys include cycling from Texas to Alaska along the spine of the Rockies, exploring climate change; and the Gyre to Gaia ocean plastic pollution sailing voyage with Pangaea Exploration. Her book, *The Carbon Cycle; Crossing the Great Divide*, was shortlisted for the 2012 Banff Mountain Festival Adventure Travel Award.

Read more at www.outdoorphilosophy.co.uk and www.facebook.com/biodiversitybikeride and on Twitter or Instagram as @CarbonCycleKate.

Just Keep Breathing

Phebe Tempelaars

It's terrifying when your mind convinces your body that you are dying. You begin panting for breath, hands sweating and legs shaking as the palpitations pound through your body like trance music. That's just a small part of what you will feel if you have a panic attack.

I've dealt with those sudden invisible hands around my throat since puberty. They are especially likely to come during unfamiliar or stressful situations, and mostly at night. So when my friend, Maaike, proposed that we spend four days hiking in the north of Colombia, I had to take a very deep breath.

Thousands of What Ifs ran through my head. What if we get lost in the jungle? What if a spider thinks my ear is a good place to spend the night? What if we get kidnapped by guerrillas? If we get diarrhoea and there is no toilet paper left? What if we accidently offend the *cacique* (head of the indigenous tribe)? What if I step on a poisonous scorpion? My vivid imagination played out all the things that could go wrong on our trip to Ciudad Perdida, The Lost City, a name that already sounded like a warning to me.

It took several long talks before I could actually feel excited about our trip. Maaike and I had no hiking experience and we weren't that sporty, but we would do it together.

Our families were not pleased by the idea of two blonde girls hiking in a jungle full of terror. The Colombia they had seen on the eight o'clock European news is a country filled with drugs, guerrillas, kidnapping, murder and corruption. You have to be a strong parent to kiss your daughter goodbye at the airport, believing she is going to one of the most dangerous countries in South America.

I made preparations to stave off the panic. I made sure I had relaxing music and an extra phone charger so I'd be as reachable as possible. I packed homeopathic anti-stress pills as well as stronger medication that could knock me to sleep within seconds if I had a severe attack.

Maaike wanted to know exactly how she could help. I told her she would need to reassure me and tell me that nothing is wrong, that heart attacks are not common in healthy, young women. I explained that she could hug me to help me return to the real world, and that it is especially important to remind me to breathe out.

I also told her that humour would help, an idea she took very seriously. "I will start looking for some funny stories and practice my comedy skills," she said. In itself, Maaike's determination to be funny made me laugh, and I thought "Everything will be fine."

We were as prepared as we could be, and ready to start the hike. Seaside gave way to dark green mountains as we bumped our way through stunning views. Our guide Camacho dropped us off at a town called Machete. "Get ready, eat well, go to the toilet and be ready in one hour," he said. The restaurant – both a start and end point for the hike – was filled with a mixture of excited newcomers and unwashed, stinky returners.

It was difficult to swallow my doubts, especially when Camacho warned us about some of the dangers. "Always use a flashlight in the evening and be alert for animals. Check your shoes for scorpions in the morning. Never wander around by yourself, follow the path and make sure you drink enough water," he instructed. The nerves were tickling my belly. I sent a quick message to my parents: In case I don't return, I love you (wink). Just what they wanted to hear before their daughter lost phone reception for four days.

We set off after lunch. Our guide, armed with a knife, showed us a map of the Sierra Nevada and explained where we would sleep. All I saw was a huge green overview with several lines, and I thought: it can't be that hard.

An hour later I found myself so tired, thirsty and frustrated that I wanted to cry. In my mind I cried like a baby. Humans these days are not meant to hike for hours and hours. Modern people should stay in hotels, get drunk on cheap beer and take salsa classes. Who came up with the crazy idea to walk and walk and walk for fun? How am I ever going to reach that hidden city? And what about Maaike, who always said she was not very fit but is now at the front of the group?

I guess my breakdown came a bit earlier than expected.

But then, in the shadow of the jungle, after losing two litres of sweat, I started to enjoy the adventure. I gazed at the palm trees and the bamboo creeks and listened to the sounds of nature. I changed my mindset and focused on putting one foot in front of the other until we reached a rest point, where there was juicy watermelon waiting for us. Maaike gave me a pep talk and off we went again. "There are a lot of animals here: tropical birds, monkeys, even pumas," Camacho said. Say what? Pumas were definitely not part of the itinerary. With a big smile and a fatherly hand on my shoulder he assured me that the pumas were more scared of me then I was of them. I smiled back at him, thinking: speak for yourself, you are the one with the knife. My mosquito repellent was effective against flying insects, but a puma would laugh and use it as perfume as he polished off the last of my bones.

As we ventured deeper into the woods we saw Kogi indigenous people, their long black hair in stark contrast to their white clothing. Directly descended from the Tairona

civilisation, their culture has hardly changed in five centuries. At times hunted and enslaved, the tribe has faced discrimination, torture, and the destruction and commercialisation of their land. It's humbling to see how they

155

have held onto their traditional way of life, living in harmony with nature. They were not keen on contact, and I realised we had to respect that we were in their territory, visiting their villages, stepping on their doorsteps. Just getting a glimpse of that ancient culture made all the sweat, blisters, breakdowns and sunburns worthwhile.

It was late in the afternoon when we dipped our toes into a natural swimming pool close to the camp. The first touch of cool water felt like heaven. The creek was surrounded by metre-high rocks covered with moss. It was like a scene from Jurassic Park, with green-blue hummingbirds flying around instead of dinosaurs. My legs were tired and burning, but the water did its job. I looked up at the clear sky and the climbing liana vines hanging from the trees, took a deep breath, and laughed. We had made it through our first day.

My relief was quickly overshadowed by the powerful voice of anxiety that said "You're in the middle of the jungle and you might get a panic attack tonight. Everybody will laugh at you. There are no ambulances or doctors here, only slow donkeys." Luckily, a yell from Maaike pulled me out of my worried brain as she jumped clumsily into the dark blue water. I giggled; she always makes me laugh.

Nature had another gift in store for us after sunset – a dazzling sky filled with stars. We filled our hungry bellies with traditional Colombian rice with chicken, fried plantain and beans. Candlelight on the tables lent a special elegance to the dinner as we bonded with our fellow travellers. Introductions were made and stories were told, until our eyes started to close and everybody made their way to bed.

That's when my struggle started. It was night and I was in the middle of nowhere, in an unknown place with no way to make contact with the outside world. Maaike hugged me and assured me that I could always wake her up if I needed her.

As soon as my head touched the pillow, my heart started pounding. It pounded so hard and fast that I could feel the blood streaming in my ears. The shaking had already started.

Cold sweat appeared on my forehead. I begged myself: please, please, don't let the panic take over.

My mind tricks my body into acting as if my life is in danger. It can last for anything from a few minutes to a few hours as an overwhelming fear takes over and I become convinced that I am dying. In that moment, I feel more alone than I have ever felt.

"No," I told myself, "I am not letting this happen." I took a few deep breaths and focused on the sounds of snoring people, soft voices in the background and the chirping of what seemed like an orchestra of crickets. Far away, water rippled in a calming rhythm. And something unexpected happened. I was enveloped by a sense of security. My heart calmed down, my breath became stable and I fell into a deep sleep.

"Get up, time to wake up," shouted our guide, who did not seem quite so lovely right then. It was four o'clock in the morning and his shouts were echoed by the sounds of pots and pans being slammed together. Growling, I stepped out of bed, checking my shoes for scorpions or spiders. As I took in the fairy tale skyline, I realised it was one of the most magical wake ups of my life.

A huge, arrogant toad stared at me on my way to the toilet and croaked. "Morning mister toad," I greeted him. It was funny to share this momentous new day with an unimpressed toad. Something had clicked inside me and I was not afraid anymore. My life has been free from panic attacks ever since.

I have learned to just keep breathing.

Phebe Tempelaars

Phebe is a Dutch foreign correspondent who considers it her job to draw a true picture of Latin America. She is frustrated to see so much bad news about the region in the European headlines and knows there is more to Latin America than drugs, corruption and murder. She believes travel makes humanity more sympathetic and can help provide a voice for those who are not often heard. She believes women should be safe to travel wherever they choose and motivating women to cross literal and figurative boundaries will contribute to a more understanding world. Find Phebe's work at www.wordcatch-journalism.com and follow her on Twitter: @ptempelaars.

If you have had similar experiences and want to connect with Phebe, contact her at wordcatchjournalism@gmail.com.

We Hadn't Even Said Hello

Paula Veselovschi

The Buenos Aires shantytowns slid before my eyes as if on a TV screen. As we were leaving the city, a man got on the bus at the last moment and quietly took the seat next to me. From where I was, I could see his worn but polished shoes, his old jeans, his big, wrinkled hands.

"I went to Santa Rosa this weekend. To meet a twenty-nine year-old daughter I didn't even know I had."

I turned my head and took a closer look at him. He had greying hair and delicate features, contrasting with his overall rugged appearance.

"I have three more children," he said. "My oldest son now lives in Santiago del Estero and the middle daughter in Gualeguayuchú. Manuel, the youngest one, died in 2002 in a motorbike accident. He was seventeen."

His voice was trembling.

I sat in silence, nested in the warmth of my seat, not knowing where to look or what to say. We hadn't even said hello to each other.

"Sorry, can I just adjust the curtains?" I asked, and I rose to pull the blinds without waiting for his answer. "The light is strong at this time of the day."

"Sure, go ahead."

We were seated in the first row of the upper deck and the cold, blinding winter sun was shining directly upon us through the front window.

"She contacted me about a month ago. Her mother did, actually. For the first time after our affair had ended. Then I went through some paternity tests and they turned out positive, so two weeks ago I rode to Santiago and to Gualeguayuchú to tell my other kids about their sister. This type of news, you know, can't be delivered over the phone. And they were happy. Really, really happy."

He paused.

"Finding out about her, thirteen years after the death of my son is… it's just an extraordinary gift."

I looked at him again. His face was beaming with what seemed to be a state of perfect, unshakable bliss.

"And where are you going now?"

"I'm going home, to Gualeguay, about seven hours from here," he answered. "The last ten days have been hectic – the trips to see my children, and this one to Santa Rosa to meet my daughter. It was wonderful, but I'm a bit tired. What about you?"

"To Puerto Iguazu, I'm heading to see the falls. They're spectacular, right?"

"I don't know," he said. "I've never been there."

The bus sped along the highway, leaving behind cheap motels and roadside shacks selling fish from the Paraná River. Hours passed, and the harsh midday sun grew milder and milder. Buenos Aires was now far behind.

I was coming from a particularly painful time in my life. During a year in Chile, I had spent Christmas by myself, New Year's Eve in bed, my days at the office, and my weekends at home. A move gone wrong, personally and professionally, had left me feeling lonelier than I had ever been. Instead of fighting it, I packed my bags and took to the road. Alone.

The Argentine pampa lay in front of my eyes, immense. Flat. Desolate.

"I think I'm going to bring her to our next family reunion. Now she's one of us," he said. "Every year we get together, and sometimes up to three thousand people show up."

"Three thousand?"

"We are the descendants of Italian immigrants who came to Argentina around 1880. Italy was a pretty crammed place back then, while here the land was plentiful and the soil fertile. What more could they have asked for? So they settled and started having children. Eight, nine, ten per family. And then the children grew up, and had eight or nine children themselves, and so on. Now yes, we're about three thousand. You can't imagine how different the people at these reunions can be: fair-skinned, dark-skinned, hard workers, black sheep, artists, clowns, rich people, poor people. Of course, the number includes the spouses and kids, even the in-laws in some cases. But that's okay. Everybody's welcome. We're happy to have each other," he smiled. "And you? What about your family?"

"Oh. We're just three," I answered, almost apologizing. "My parents and I. No brothers, no sisters, no aunts or uncles or cousins or anything. Just the three of us. No need for special reunions."

I lifted my shoulders in a shrug.

"A tiny family indeed. You know why here in Argentina families are so strong? It's because if you come to this wilderness with no possessions and nobody else to have a word with for miles and miles, family does become the only shelter you have. Both from wind and from solitude. You don't need that in Europe."

We don't.

I looked out of the window. The naked plain surrounded us like a quiet, grey ocean. An ocean which bore no traces of myself, which shared none of my history, but in which a hundred and thirty years before a handful of Italian immigrants had arrived, built their first homes and had their first children. A tamed space in which the old man next to me found warmth, comfort and a pair of loving eyes wherever he turned his gaze.

Ever since I started traveling, safety has been less of a

concern than connection. It's never easy chatting to strangers, let alone opening up. Yet time and time again, a mysterious angel of solitary travelers ensured that fleeting bonds tied me to places in ways that I could never have anticipated. I unexpectedly found shelter through vulnerability, and connection through isolation. All I had to do was listen.

The sky turned purple as the sun set against a distant row of leafless trees. Lights were coming on in all directions, showing us that we were getting close to a village, or maybe to a town.

The bus soon entered the terminal of Gualeguay.

"I'm getting off here, it was a pleasure to meet you, young lady."

"A pleasure to meet you too. Goodbye!"

"Goodbye."

He walked away. I watched him go, and realized that he hadn't even told me his name.

But it was pointless to ask. We hadn't even said hello.

Paula Veselovschi

Paula is originally from Romania and fell in love with Latin America in 2011. Her travels for work, study and discovery have taken her from Mexico to the south of Argentina, passing through more than ten countries along the way. Paula delights in learning about the intricate realities of Latin America and hearing the original ideas of the region's thinkers of all ages, nationalities and walks of life. She travels slowly and is currently based in Bogota, Colombia where she investigates issues relating to sustainability and writes about her experiences, mostly in Romanian, on her blog www.latinoamericando.ro.

A Face at the Window

Ailana Navarez

In the 1960s and 1970s Contadora Island, off Panama's Pacific coast, was the hush-hush getaway of Hollywood celebrities, local aristocrats and the exiled Shah of Iran. In the 80s it was a negotiating headquarters for resolving civil wars in Central America and the Panama Canal treaty. In the 90s and early 2000s, it was the home of a Colombian drug lord and political aristocrat who transformed a so-called seven-star hotel into a money laundering outpost, running it and the island's infrastructure into the ground.

As a child growing up there, I only knew it as home.

As a young woman returning to visit, I realized it not only represented Latin America's socio-economic and political imperfections, but the perfect imperfections of being a woman traveling solo. More than a decade separated my childhood on Contadora Island and my return as a young woman. During that decade I lived and traveled to other countries with family, moved back to the United States, attended university, and became a journalist.

My initial return to Panama was as a deputy editor for a newspaper, with a possible offer to be the campaign manager for a local politician too. After further investigation and gentle advice from several people, I realized that those opportunities would not support the life paths I was striving for as a student, future professional, and overall patriotic American. I vowed to return to the United States, gain more skills, give back to my country, and return to Latin America when a better quality of life – and actually having a life – would be more feasible.

Until then, there was one last thing I had to do before leaving the nation of my childhood for what could plausibly be many more years. I was grateful my remaining travel budget afforded me the chance to connect again more deeply with my former home – Contadora Island, a pearl of safety in an otherwise ever-changing, dog-eat-dog country.

I remember interviewing a high-ranked Panama Canal security official in Casco Viejo. We discussed the way Panama walks a tightrope between first, second and third world countries, as well as its unique multi-cultural and geostrategic position in the twenty-first century. In retrospect, what struck me most was not his opinions on his country, but the way he acted towards me as a woman. I have experienced much worse. I have been cornered by men in favelas and driven in cars by gun-toting strangers who could have snapped my body like a toothpick. No one would have known where to begin looking for me, because these men were above the law.

This was more psychological. With the slime of a been-there, done-that Cold War veteran and the confidence of a *machista*, the senior official made it clear that he did not respect or recognize the possibility of a woman traveling alone.

"Women don't do things alone here," he argued. He leaned in with a smirk to add, "Different always gets you in trouble."

I grew up in Latin America and have made some very adventurous travel decisions. I fully comprehend the real vulnerabilities of being a globetrotting, independent woman. But I am also someone who doesn't like things getting in my way.

In this case, I responded with diplomacy, recognizing that the catcalls that met me outside the restaurant and the comments of that slimy official within came from exactly the same type of thinking. But it made me look forward to the safety of Contadora Island even more.

Boarding the rickety plane on a former U.S. air base, my backpack and I settled behind a group of Argentinians. Having lived in Uruguay, I enjoyed hearing the local dialect again. I was also reminded of the underlying *machismo* of the southern cone giant compared with its tiny, more gender-equality focused neighbor. Loud bickering dominated the flight as the Argentinian men in front taunted their partners. Then, at the point where the women had had enough and become furious, the men kissed them and all was forgiven. The women were so willing to give in that the cycle just kept repeating.

The rest of the passengers and I sat in quiet amusement at first, then I felt frustrated. It is difficult to know when to help other women or when to let them be. Is it the world they have chosen, one that has been chosen for them, or a mix? Would help have diminished the drama or overarching objectification dynamic?

After being in Panama City and David – where development is skyrocketing, but the city is still sketchy – landing in safe, tiny Contadora Island was a breath of fresh air. We now rent out the family house, and when I got there I met the manager again for the first time since we left. Nostalgically, I thought he looked the same, as did much of the island's infrastructure despite newly paved roads and residential complexes. Our house also looked nearly identical. It was a beach house from the dictatorship era where the simple, colorful design and barred windows were a security plus. Let the robbers pick on someone who seemed more wealthy and less security savvy. The rental manager had suggested we update the house to twenty-first century aesthetics. While the island was now much safer after its difficult era, that did not change my security-first instincts. I had no idea that those instincts would be proved right within a matter of hours.

Next stop, the famous – and now infamous – Hotel Contadora, the former seven-star hotel that had been taken over by the Colombian drug lord.

As a child, I remember its grand dining hall where my family had dinner with friends and business associates, as well as its pools, the exotic zoo, golf courses and a private beach.

Returning to it years later, the situation was just the opposite. A decaying ferry boat at the end of the long white sand beach symbolized one of the legendary hotel's less fortunate ventures.

After the hotel's Colombian manager was killed in a mysterious plane crash, a combination of family feuds, Russian investors, and tax problems destroyed what was left of the hotel. Anyone in the area with a pickup truck or boat stripped the hotel's remaining grandeur. My family even has some wood carvings, stationary and tables from the property, although that was the least of its riches. Now it is a skeleton of the past, and instead of attracting tourists to stay in its lush rooms, they come to take photos of the vine-covered ruins.

Sadly, tourists aren't the only ones to be drawn to the dilapidated buildings. It is also the headquarters of a much less nostalgic and insecure present – narco-trafficking.

Midday arrived and pasty tourists on the hotel beach began returning to their air-conditioned hotel rooms elsewhere. I was well aware of the dangers of being there alone and planned to leave sooner rather than later.

Then pickup truck after pickup truck began arriving on the scene filled with armed men, followed by an expensive imported car. Here I was, a lone woman in a bikini, taking photos with an expensive imported camera and a decreasing number of witnesses. The pickup trucks contained stuffed black bags and were circling at the back of the hotel. Instinct kicked in and I hid.

I moved toward my ATV in the front of the hotel. The aged vehicle had a faulty engine and proved to be no stealth machine. I cranked it. A group of men began approaching. I gassed it out of there.

It was a close call, but that's the type of thing that can happen when travelers venture beyond their gated communities, cosseted tours and guarded resorts that are so unrepresentative of the developing countries they are visiting. All the same, I was relieved to get away and later met up with some old friends. We shared stories about all the things I had missed.

That experience was still with me when I got back to the house, especially as I was there alone. I knew the drill – it's better to be safe than sorry, regardless of where you are. I closed all the drapes of the barred windows, locked the doors and turned the TV on low. The gentle breeze meant I didn't need to crank the air conditioner. I sat in the open living and dining room, facing my laptop's screen light away from any angle of visibility from the windows, with music on but not loud enough for it to be heard outside.

I was video calling my boyfriend when I noticed people lurking outside. They crept through the rocks and grass. They were trying to be quiet, but I could hear them whispering and testing the doors. At first, I rationalized that this was my mind making things up because I was alone – it's not unusual to hear animal noises in the night. Unfortunately, even on Contadora Island, it's also not unusual to find a strange man's face looking straight in between the gap in the curtains.

I acted fast.

I grabbed my laptop and camera and locked myself in the back bedroom. My boyfriend was freaking out more than I was. I signed off, telling him it was nothing, even though the words felt hollow and what I actually wanted was for someone to reassure me. I used furniture to barricade the doors. I warded off panic with action: I called the police. No answer. Then I remembered the island no longer had police – just an anti-narcotics force. Earlier in the day my island friends had joked – with some truth – that "they're not here

to protect the people, just the black bags."

So I called the rental manager. No reply. Then suddenly a text: "I'll be right there." The manager arrived and assured me that things like that rarely happened here, but he still offered me a place in another rental with more people.

Upon returning to Panama City, a friend who had worked on the island suggested that I might have been at risk because

I'd witnessed the armed men with black bags. Alternatively, it was known that some of the increasing numbers of poor workers arriving from the mainland try to occupy uninhabited homes. Whoever they were, and whatever their intentions, it had been the type of surprise moment of vulnerability that no solo traveler wants to encounter.

Not only was it upsetting to discover how the black bags had become rife in the supposedly safe island of my childhood home, it also made me think about the risks that we continue to take traveling alone.

For me, the reasons why you should not go it alone are always outnumbered by the reasons why you should. Traveling solo teaches us about ourselves and the places and people we encounter. My experiences on Contadora Island were an example of the ways that dreams, fears and hopes collide and unite when we travel.

Ailana Navarez

Ailana is the editor-in-chief of *Pulsamerica*. She has published more than seventy international relations-related articles as a political analyst/journalist focused on Latin American leadership analysis, commerce, government, history, international relations, narco-trafficking and security. As a photographer she has covered summits, protests, environmental affairs, and political campaigns. She is Harvard University educated in Government and Psychology and certified in counter-terrorism. She maintains permanent residency status in Panama, the USA, and Uruguay and speaks English, Spanish, Portuguese, and Hawaiian Creole. Ailana enjoys travel, horseback riding, Muay Thai, Krav Maga, yoga, drawing, being a history buff, reading, and keeping in touch with friends and family.

Day One Hundred and Twenty Two

Emma Murray

I'm sitting on the tile floor of Pablo Neruda's home on Isla Negra, the poet's coastal hermitage, and there's pear juice dripping down my knee. It's the third, and last, of Pablo's houses-turned-museums that I'll visit. The other two – one in Santiago and one in Valparaíso – I ambled through last week, pausing to stare at the ceilings that he and his wild-haired mistress stared at before falling asleep, toeing the cement cracks his toes brushed a thousand times, letting my fingers linger on the doorknob he palmed over and over again to reach fresh air. Isla Negra was his getaway, an escape from his turbulent, politically-charged world.

As the pear's juice crawls to my ankle, I tuck its core into my bag. Tour groups in large clusters file in and out, and amidst their hubbub I realize I need to leave and find the beach, which you can see from Pablo's living room: A swath of icy Pacific sprawling towards the horizon and a handful of SUV-sized black rocks resting in the sand.

I walk a dirt path to the big blocks and run my fingertips along the rough grooves. I start to climb, then sit perched atop the tallest one. In my four months of travel I've realized I do my best thinking when I'm alone.

I have a lot to think about.

Above me, the sky is stormy and grey. I wrap my rain jacket tighter and stare into the ocean. The escaped hair from my ponytail whips my ear and I curl my knees into my chest. The waves' constant rolling and breaking and rolling and breaking and rolling hypnotizes me. Blues and greys collide with browns and greens, and a magnificent white foam erupts, bubbling against the dark sand.

I feel the shift: one plus one equals three. Blue and brown make white. Time can stop. Empty really means full. This moment is what I've come here for; this is why I left.

I feel your eyes travel, I feel him carve the letters in the sand, *and distant is the autumn: a grey beret, a bird's voice, and the heart of a house to where my deepest longings elope and my kisses land joyously like glowing embers.*[1]

A group of school-aged kids run over and stomp across the ground beneath my rock. I wonder if they know I'm sitting, seagull-like, up here. They continue on and I turn my attention back west, devote my gaze to the waves, let them incorporate me into this infinite space to which I've been transported.

In my hypnosis I travel back, connecting with Pablo, feeling the inspiration he felt looking at these waves. Same play, different actors.

I feel what Pablo felt: The invigorating, yet calming contrast between the ocean, sand, and giant black rocks, and the warm evergreen trees and the house behind us. I feel connected and re-rooted to the world.

Six months ago, I was walking across Brown University's campus center, staring down at my palms. I was two exams away from ending my sophomore year and my fingers wouldn't stop trembling. They were like pent up puppies. Keyboards, multi-colored highlighters, my iPhone screen, a dining hall fork, thin pages of Kant, Foucault, Neruda, García Márquez, Dillard, Kerouac weren't enough. We needed more exercise, more room to roam.

Studying philosophy and literature had elevated my brain, but then ditched it up in the clouds. I'd forgotten why I was there and where I was going. What good was a winning argument for morality when I couldn't contextualize it in real life? Where did these words that I obsessed over come from? Why did they come to be? What did they really mean? What was my place in their, or rather, any existence?

The hundreds of pages I read each week, the thousands of words I tried to capture, the concepts I struggled to grasp, and the social dorm life I barely managed to juggle left me no time to figure these things out. My chronic to-do list wouldn't let me sit still.

So I left. Alone. I bought a one-way ticket to Ecuador, and now, months later, I'm sitting on this rock, an hour's hitchhike west of Santiago. I've read more for-pleasure books, written more meaningful words, met more compatible people, and explored more of myself since I arrived than in the previous two years.

I came here to learn what I could not learn while tethered down by assignments and the weight of societal expectations. I came here to taste the space you need for true aloneness. I stayed here to choreograph the dance between my passions and my skills.

I first read Pablo when I was in fifth grade. We made drawings of artichokes, *alcachofas*, and I first learned about abstract concepts like metaphors and similes. *Leaf after leaf*, he writes, I read, *we undress the delicacy and eat the peaceful body of its green heart.*[2]

Pablo knows intimately the potential of an honorable life well lived. It's a mix of loud and soft, right and wrong, past and present. A delicate balance. A dance, just like the waves.

Overlooking the stormy Pacific, I feel my love for literature, *español*, freedom, curiosity, inspiration, Pablo, the soulful, brave, nature, and love itself all braid themselves into a harmony that I feel resonate from my fingertips to my toes. *Beyond your eyes the twilight burns. Dry leaves of autumn twist in your soul.*[3] I am alive.

By going out there to the restless, fresh ocean, I find the start. I came here to taste the authenticity of the concepts I'd been fed, to touch the textile truths of the past, to find these things you cannot glean from the confines of classrooms nor from the facade of crisp, typed textbook words.

Rain starts to splatter and I jump back down. I run my fingers through the foam. The ocean is only fresh on the dunes of the shore.

Emma Murray

Emma is an award-winning adventure writer and all-around mountain lover. Her work has appeared in the pages of *Alpinist, Bivy Tales, Boulder Weekly, REI's Co-op Journal, Rock and Ice*, and *College Outside*, among others. She currently lives in Boulder, Colorado, USA, where you can find her running dirt paths or scaling vertical rock when she's not behind a keyboard or curled up with a book. Read more of Emma's writing at www.emmaathenamurray.com and follow her on Instagram: @emmaathenamurray.

[1] *Pablo Neruda (1924). Veinte poemas de amor y una canción desesperada: Poema 6. Santiago de Chile: Editorial Nascimento.*

[2] *Pablo Neruda (1954). Odas elementales: Oda a la alcachofa. Buenos Aires: Editorial Losada.*

[3] *Pablo Neruda (1924). Veinte poemas de amor y una canción desesperada: Poema 6. Santiago de Chile. Editorial Nascimento.*

The Hangover

Charlotte Mackenzie de Urrea

"You were brought in last night, no documents, either of you. Do you know how you were admitted?"

The clock on the blue wall behind the police officer filled the silence with its sharp little ticks. Even Jesus looked disinterested, hanging on his tired-looking cross next to a shabby framed photograph of President Kirchner.

"I already told you," I said. "It's our first time in Salta. We were celebrating my friend's birthday. The next thing I knew, I woke up here. I'm sure they put something in our drinks, I can even tell you which bar we went to…"

The commissariat had a kind face but his patience was wearing thin. He had better things to do at eight o'clock on a Saturday morning than listen to a gringa.

"My colleague will accompany you back to your hostel," he said, rising from his seat. "Are you okay to walk? Or would you rather we drove you?"

I decided to walk, hanging my head in shame as I wandered the dusty streets and trailed the police sergeant who had been given the onerous task of escorting me. Salta was just waking up. The streets were dusty and stray dogs loped the pavements, sniffing hopefully at the rubbish bags. Bolivian women sold empanadas stuffed with eggs, alpaca meat and rice, flashing their ankles beneath their coloured skirts. Argentinian stallholders and shopkeepers prepared their wares for yet another Saturday and little old ladies cleaned the streets outside their homes, leaving me to dodge the suds and sluices of water.

Salta is everywhere but nowhere. Like all border towns, it is somewhere in between.

I berated myself as my feet slapped along in my flip-flops. This wasn't how it was supposed to be. I had saved for weeks, learned self-defence, taken Red Cross first aid classes, and packed door locks and sterile needles. I'd left England with a backpack I could barely carry. I had begun in sprawling, grimy Buenos Aires and planned to travel through Chile and Bolivia and then onto Peru. I had felt fearless, sometimes scared, but mostly just emancipated at being so far from the unassuming calm of British society. A decade later, I wish I could warn my then nineteen-year-old self that the yellow butterflies, Eva Peróns and Inca warriors of her daydreams were a far cry from this continent of endless motion and noise. It was my first big solo adventure, and I had messed up.

I looked down at my arm where I had ripped out the IV tube with a satisfying pop that morning. I'm fine, I'm checking myself out of this dump of a hospital, my addled brain had insisted. I caught a glimpse of the large sticky-grey mark on my arm as we passed a shop window. The fibrous hairs of the sticky tape were stuck to my forearm like a weird second-skin. It was a horrible reminder of my night spent institutionalised.

"I was so worried," the hostel receptionist said. "Where have you been?"

I told her I thought our drinks had been spiked.

"I'm not sure about that," she said. "I mean, the drinks are stronger here in Argentina. Maybe you had a bit more than you intended? Don't worry, I'm glad you're both okay."

I called the hospital from an Internet café. After two long brrrings, the switchboard operator answered.

"I'm looking for my sister," I lied. "I think she was admitted last night... she's blonde, she has curly hair. Yes... yes... you pumped her stomach?"

I returned to the hospital eager to collect my friend, my companion. She was still in her own date drug world, barely coherent and unable to walk without support. She seemed pleased to see me, her partner in crime, and we left the hospital together, blinking in the midday sun. Her head lolled on my shoulder.

"You need to make a statement. Don't you realise how serious this is?" It was a different officer the second time and her disgust was evident. We stood in front of the scuffed wooden table in Salta's main police station like two schoolgirls hauled in front of the headmaster. We were both visibly shaken by our experiences the night before. The officer was unimpressed.

"We had our drinks spiked," I repeated. My friend was no help, she was still in her own sozzled little world.

"You drank too much, it's incredibly irresponsible," the officer snarled. She could barely look at us and kept her focus on ensuring we completed the forms correctly, signing our lives away in the police station's dog-eared ledger.

It was the Virgin Mary who hung above the officer's head this time, gazing at us in disapproval as I cried and muttered my excuses. It was the hangover from hell, a sorry tale that just kept on giving, reaffirming the Argentine perception of the youth of today, loose foreign women who go out and shamefacedly paint the town red. Disastrous, disgraceful, disgusting. Where are their morals? Where are their standards? What on earth would their parents say?

I was consumed by the most hideous part of any hangover, the guilt that forces you to analyse your behaviour from the previous night. It could have been so much worse. We could have been robbed, we could have been raped, or we could have been cut up into tiny pieces and minced into empanada filling. Okay, maybe that last one is a bit farfetched but, even so, we had been so lucky.

I started to experience flashbacks. We had been out celebrating my co-traveller's birthday, her twenty-first no less. Two footloose and fancy-free women on a girls' night in Salta. What could possibly go wrong? Fuelled by high spirits and cheap alcohol, we had ended up in a bar, perched on high stools as the bartender offered us a celebratory shot of tequila. The rest of the night came in flashes. There was the birthday girl lying on a metal hospital table, the yellow strip lights illuminating yet another depiction of the Virgin Mary. There was me, interrupting my friend's peace as screams and sobs wracked my body and a nurse tried to hold me back. What are you doing to her? Why isn't she moving? Where are you taking her? Then there was that last image as I blinked myself awake under my own fluorescent strip lights, an IV tube plugged into my arm.

Our experience at the main police station soured matters. I was supposed to look after my friend on her birthday, not see her interned in Salta's medical system. Her hangover guilt manifested itself in rage. I asked if she would tell her parents. She grunted in reply.

I decided to go horse riding for the afternoon. I figured it was exactly what I needed after a night spent in hospital. I went to a farm and a friendly redheaded woman greeted me. Her British accent was a welcome reminder of home.

"What's wrong with your arm?" she said. "Are you okay to ride?"

I vomited out the events of the night before.

"Friend's birthday… drink spiked… I've been in hospital… I'm fine now."

"You need a gentle horse," she said.

The awaiting *gauchos* languished around the remnants of their lunch. An overweight and optimistic Labrador slobbered around, hunting for scraps. The people had kind faces, their skin weathered by the seasons and life on this outpost, caring for herds of sheep and cattle on Argentina's 'bad lands'. My horse, as promised, was a gentleman. I made a complete mess of strapping on my leather chaps and hoisting myself into the saddle, but he didn't grumble once. He just waited for me to make myself less like a sack of potatoes.

We plodded across the pampa and I drank in the sky. Even the clouds seemed closer. In this, the cowboys' world, I was just a speck of nothingness on the horizon. A horse and his shoddy rider, trekking the plains, lost in the expanse of their surroundings. In the grand scheme of things, I was insignificant. This thought gave me a sense of relief. I glanced down at my arm, the remnants of the sticky tape now a disconcerting shade of black.

I can't claim the riding gave me an epiphany, nor did it help my throbbing head, but being so far removed from the bars and seedy clubs of Salta did make me smile, albeit weakly, by the end of the afternoon. Plodding along under those endless skies gave me time to reflect too. The non-judgemental company and my trusty horse helped me process what had happened and work out how I was going to call home and explain. No, it wasn't our fault. No, I'm not coming home. Yes, everything will be alright.

Being drugged is a primal experience. The flashbacks haunt you for years afterwards. Certain smells continue to make you nauseous and cause your palms to sweat. Tears are inevitable and so is the feeling that your privacy was compromised, that a stranger got too close. There's anger too. You berate yourself for not being more aware. I believe our drinks were spiked with a drug called Rohypnol, legal across parts of Mexico and South America. It's odourless and colourless, easy to blend into salt and drinks. It not only causes confusion and visual disturbances, it will eventually knock you out.

I didn't keep in touch with my friend. I guess that's not much of a surprise, given what had happened. We returned to the sleepy village of Pisco Elqui in Chile, where I was living and teaching English. In the weeks that followed I felt dumped as a friend, replaced by new volunteers who were apparently much savvier than my teenage self. After all, I was the one who had got us into that mess. The one who had spoiled a twenty-first birthday celebration.

Was it my fault for leading us into a dark bar, an irresponsible act in a strange place thousands of miles from home? Should we have even gone out that night to celebrate?

Would it have happened if we had been men?

Yes, we let our guard down. Yes, accepting a drink from a bartender was probably not the wisest move. But should two solo women, travelling without a chaperone, instantly be fair game? We were relaxed, happy and enjoying the festive atmosphere of Salta on a Friday night. Our behaviour was far from sexual. You might think a night out in Latin America is different from a night out elsewhere, but did we really deserve to get our drinks spiked?

Charlotte Mackenzie de Urrea

Charlotte is a self-confessed Latinophile. She has travelled Latin America extensively and lived in both Chile and Colombia. An ex-journalist, Charlotte cut her teeth writing about oil and gas and covered Venezuela and Colombia as a commodities correspondent. She edited the online publication Latin Correspondent before moving into communications. Charlotte has freelanced for publications including *LatinoLife* magazine, *Sounds and Colours*, *World Politics Review*, *Farmfolio* and *The Bogotá Post*. She married her husband, Ricardo, a true *bogotano*, in October 2016. They divide their time between London, England, and Colombia, and are already planning their next trip.

My Polola

Megan Lawton

There is a lengthy story to be told of how two fiercely independent women from different countries managed to meet each other, travel together, fall in love and cohabitate. This story begins and ends with Latin America.

Traveling is exhilarating and exhausting, a whirlwind that changes as quickly as you allow it. As a solo woman, it can be distressing (where do I buy tampons?) and hilariously stereotypical (sleeping with the surf instructor, returning to ensure a repeat experience). It can be threatening and it can be redeeming. Even the weather is unpredictable, insisting on a downpour two hours after a sandstorm, which was precluded by 102°F heat. As a woman, you meet people interested in you for less than admirable reasons, and those who are determined to assist you when something as inane as not having a ten-cent coin to enter a bus station threatens to derail your trip.

But we did it. We pushed through the anxiety and the elation, the ebbs and the flows and we found each other in Paracas, an alluring Peruvian beach town. On the backpacker trail for its epic sand dunes and nature reserve, there's not much else to do in Paracas but laze and drink Peruvian pisco (never to be confused with Chilean pisco).

There we were. Two single women on two lengthy expeditions through South America. Both with a sense of wanderlust that had led us to this very cosmic place, Inca lines included.

People who are used to navigating alone are naturally

apprehensive at the thought of doing it together. But forces of nature are hard to ignore and it was together that we arrived at one of our first mishaps. A misadventure involving a seemingly romantic picnic invaded by a drunken local man. What had seemed like it would end in a homophobic attack resulted in nothing more than a stolen wheel of cheese. The distinctive and mouthwatering cheese of Arequipa, Peru, but cheese nevertheless.

Being gay in Bolivia didn't seem like the optimal situation either, but that wasn't the cause of our problems. Instead we had punishing stomach ailments to contend with, along with stolen money and missing phones. We spent Valentine's Day in La Paz, attempting to do the classic backpacker 'best food, cheapest price' charade. That endeavor led to two hours spent walking the city's ominously polluted streets.

These are stories I would be without had I carried on my path alone. These are anecdotes that could have had far worse outcomes too. They could have been stories tainted by Latin America's deeply Christian and supposedly visceral response to lesbians, for example.

Instead, they are stories of sunsets and twenty hours spent hitchhiking down the Chilean coast with friends we had made on the road. They are memories of hiking to near death in the Colca Canyon, spurred on by our iPods and never faltering reggaeton playlists, of sleeping in a hilltop radio tower overlooking an obscure Bolivian town, of volunteering in hostels, where we answered doors in the middle of the night as we drank forgotten backpacker wine.

They are stories of riding bikes, and eating exquisite seafood soup for US$2, and drinking sickeningly sweet *terremotos* (let's hope Chile doesn't go down in history for mixing ice-cream and wine) and then there is our story, of how we found jobs and settled into our new life in Santiago.

I wouldn't have this version of my life if I hadn't met my

comrade, my *polola*. If I hadn't uprooted my life to venture to Latin America alone and unsuspecting. As Mexican poet Amado Nervo once said, "Don't stop the woman who leaves nor the bird that flies; let fate take its course."

And so it has.

Megan Lawton

Megan is originally from a small but touristy beach town on the East Coast of the USA. She studied Geography for four years in university classrooms before she realized how important it was to personally experience her own course work. She has since travelled and lived throughout Asia and Latin America, and has dabbled in teaching English and writing along the way. She enjoys attempting elaborate hikes with little to no preparation, as well as any and all activities that involve the beach. If a beach cannot be found, a dog park will probably suffice. When *Alone Together* goes to press Megan's location will more than likely be unknown, much to her mother's chagrin.

Down the Napo River

Stephanie A. Wolcott

They call it the lungs of the Earth. The Amazon is the largest, most diverse tropical rainforest in the world. The forest spans nine countries and covers five and a half million square kilometers. This vast green organ absorbs carbon dioxide and breathes out life-giving oxygen. The metaphor of lungs of the Earth seems completely appropriate.

I landed in Quito, Ecuador, in September 2008 and decided to get my bearings by staying with a friend who worked for a nonprofit organization in the district of Guápulo. Visiting the district of Guápulo is like taking a trip down a rabbit hole. Tall, shiny office buildings line up in a row on the last flat part of Quito, before the earth takes a nosedive into Guápulo's winding cobblestone streets and centuries-old buildings. There are no flat streets. Everyone walking somewhere is either going up or going down. The steep terrain might explain why the modern buildings of Quito stopped at the ledge and never took over this quirky hamlet.

The day I arrived, a festival had just begun. It started slowly, but sped up into a whirling celebration. It began with the obligatory parade, as a statue of the mother of Jesus was carried through the streets on the shoulders of villagers. That day, Mary finished her journey at a local grocery store. I was told that on each day of the festival she would move to another store to bless it, a sort of insurance policy. In the afternoon, music started to play in the plaza in front of the small but ornate cathedral.

By evening, a crowd had gathered. Locals were joined by people who looked like they had come from the countryside. There were very short women with long braids who had cages strapped to their backs with chickens inside. The women spun to the music in hypnotic trances and I wondered how the chickens felt. Children ran around eating local sweets. The master of ceremonies had a megaphone and yelled, "*Viva Guápulo*" every ten minutes or so. Someone offered me *chicha*, a fermented corn alcohol, and I politely refused. Drinking a magic potion of mysterious origins did not seem like a good idea at a crazy village party with gorillas. Did I mention the gorillas? For reasons I do not know, quite a few people were running around in gorilla suits.

I left the party and tried to sleep. The "*Viva Guápulo*" refrain continued throughout the night and every once in a while I was awakened by homemade fireworks. In the morning my friend told me that festivals like those last for days. Even though I had just arrived, I decided it might be a good idea to leave for a bit. That is one of the benefits of traveling alone, you can be spontaneous and do what you like, when you like. I found a small travel agent that takes people down the Napo River to a remote eco-resort in the Amazon. Ecuador is a small but incredibly diverse country. You can go from the city to the deep jungle in a day, and that is what I planned to do.

I flew from Quito to Coca, a run-down town that serves as a starting point for most journeys into the Amazon. The town was built around the oil industry that has been exploiting the Amazon for decades, extracting oil, inflating the local economy and leaving an environmental mess. Whatever your perception of the role of oil in developing economies, a trip to Coca will leave you seriously questioning the degree to which extractive industries contribute to people's quality of life.

Luckily, I was only in Coca for a few hours before I boarded a large canoe with a motor at one end and headed down the Napo River. After a few hours, we reached the lodge. The first thing I noticed was the heavy, hot, humid air. Nothing ever dries, there are just degrees of wet. Hanging your towel in the sun for a day means it will be only slightly damp when you need to use it again the next morning.

I do not like heat. My skin prickles and I get stripes of sunburn if I've missed even the thinnest sliver of skin while applying sunscreen. The Amazon is brutally, oppressively hot and humid. It is full of mosquitos and seriously uncomfortable at times. However, when the going gets tough I always ask myself, "Would you rather be where you are right now, or sitting at a desk in a sterile, corporate box?"

The answer has always been, "I'd rather be here."

And "here" was not so rough – in fact, it seemed quite interesting. The resort was designed to be almost completely self-sufficient; partly out of necessity due to the remote location and partly because of a desire to not disrupt the fragile eco-system. The electricity came from solar power. Food scraps were fed to the pigs. Staff collected rainwater, grew rice and gathered fruit from the jungle. The resort had a social component too, helping to fund a nearby school where the students learned a combination of local heritage and ecotourism. That way young people could retain their culture while also taking advantage of a boom in sustainable tourism.

The whole community stood in stark contrast to Coca. Here, I saw local initiative and pride in their own version of progress. People smiled. They played soccer, swam in the river and sold me necklaces they had made with red and black seeds from the Amazon.

On the second day, the resort offered a trip to a more remote community further down the river. The people in this small village were hunter-gatherers. Their stilt houses were made of local wood strapped together. A toucan perched on the porch railing of one house, next to a little girl in a dusty t-shirt and shorts. An older man took us on a short tour, pointed out native plants and told us what they were used for. Few of us realize that a full twenty-five percent of Western pharmaceuticals are derived from rainforest materials.

I asked what was further down the river and our guide said that they do not take outsiders deeper into the Amazon. The rainforest is home to people who live off the land completely and choose to live separately. I felt privileged to have been welcomed into this community for the afternoon, but I wished to intrude no further. Not everyone enjoys sunburned white people nosing around their houses and asking where the nearest bathroom is.

The surprise of the day was that our tour guide offered us the option to float back to the resort in an inner tube. At first I refused. Rivers are home to alligators, snakes, piranhas and a host of other creatures I didn't want to encounter close up. However, the guide assured me repeatedly it would be safe, so I got into the water. The cool water felt amazing on my overheated skin. I lay on my back and the trees passing by created a hypnotic effect. It was one of those perfect travel moments, the moments that make all the crazy swirling chicken dancers, oppressive heat and exhausting travel worth it. It felt absolutely ridiculous to be drifting down the Napo fully dressed, but I enjoyed it immensely.

A few days later, I made the canoe trip and plane flight back to Quito. At the airport, I heard the news that Lehman Brothers had fallen. Lehman Brothers was the first domino of the colossal sub-prime mortgage disaster that caused so many people to lose their houses, their jobs and their life savings. Modern civilization had created a monster. We had built an economic system so complex and so detached from anything real, when it collapsed it took many people's dreams with it.

My mind returned to the people I had met in the Amazon. Could it be that they have something to teach us, and are we willing to listen?

Stephanie A. Wolcott

Stephanie wrote her story to encourage other women to book that ticket, get on the plane, test their limits, set aside their fears, and learn more about the glorious world we live in. Stephanie has traveled to remote places for both work and fun, gotten herself out of some odd situations, met fabulous people, and gained valuable perspective along the way. Two years ago she made a massive leap and moved from Chicago, USA, to Bogota, Colombia, where she is excited to be part of the rebuilding of a beautiful, ecologically and ethnically diverse country following decades of social unrest. Connect with Stephanie on LinkedIn at www.linkedin.com/in/

stephaniewolcott1/ and follow her on Twitter: @sawolcott

My Shaman

Priyanka Gupta

What is it that makes me yearn for you?
His dark blonde hair
like the soft dry golden cotton-like grass on
you,
his dark blonde eyes
like the pearls of dew, which reflect lights,
settled on the green grass blades in the cold
mornings,
his long thin legs
like the palm trees standing straight but
sometimes swinging with the wind,
his perfect smile
like the blossoming white gerbera on the
window sill
his sun-burnt nose
like the red ripe apples of summer
that I could pluck off and eat,
his pink lips that he peels
like the seasonal flowers that patted your
ground inch by inch.

It is your moons we dreamed interlocked,
it is your suns spent wandering hand in hand,

it is our smiles sprayed randomly all day long.
It is those nine months I breathed you,
it is the windy, rainy nights when the sky above
you stormed
and the roof almost fell,
it is the days when wind gushed by, whispering
in my ears,
picking up your scent in its breath
and mixing it with my skin.

What about his laser-like stares?
I didn't even know I had those layers
that he stripped away.
Sleeping in your sunshine,
I clasped him for so long.
You didn't let it rain that day.

What about those kisses?
I can still feel the first one,
he pulled me, you peeped at us,
smiling, as if you were saying,
there is more to come.
We lost identities
like the Amazon falling into the Atlantic.

It might be the food we ate together,
you gave *chicha* of the purple corn
and the cheese empanadas,
it reflected in the pink of our cheeks.

It was the fluid conversations,
he wanted to know everything about me
but he did not ask anything.
Why did you act as if I was always yours?

It was his love for stones,
the ones we robbed from your Titicaca and
Pacific,
drinking coca tea silently,
spinning at your heights,
he told me I am a part of him
like you were a part of me.

It was the separation maybe,
we were high to see each other again,
it was a mistake telling him about Shiva day,
so stoned was he that Monday,
listening to ayahuasca music,
he tranced into my shaman,
though he hasn't healed me yet.
You let it pour that day.

It was the shower of experiences,
The Dutch family, the tree house, the
Argentinian singers,
Like the countless colorful mushrooms in your
jungles,
And the numerous hummingbirds I counted in
your Amazon.
Remember, he took out the spine that you put
in my slipper?

It was him napping in my lap in the Inca ruins,
I want him that close
where I can touch his soft hair
and protect him from the sun,
by covering his face with mine
and my long dark hair,
through which he breathed.

It was the way he offered his hand,
though he knew I did not need it.
He wanted to be there for me
and then he asked if he was a man yet.
Yes, I said.

It was the gentler version of myself that I saw,
when I was with him
and you.

It was the fun stories,
like the one when we were having sex
and I googled some concepts.
He was on top and I was on the phone,
crazy random nonsense.

It was the rainy last day in Santa Cruz,
with the dinner at the shawarma place,
he wore the yellow rain jacket
and I could not keep my eyes off him.
We talked for hours

and then we found some snails on the way
back.
I had to leave the next day.
I did not have enough guts to tell my parents
that I liked you,
how unhappy we were when I left,
do you remember?

It was my tears, which fell,
glistening the autumn leaves that covered you,
making you prettier,
like my silverware,
yes, my jewelry was his silverware.

Separation has been worth it,
for both of you, it is all worth it.
And remember my love,
there is always more to come.

Priyanka Gupta

Priyanka was born in a small town in northern India. She is a software engineer by education but has been coding fictional characters since childhood. She wrote a rhyming poem about King Solomon when she was thirteen. She started her solo travels with trips in India to Kerala and Goa, then traveled Europe, Southeast Asia, and South America where travelers buzzed like bees over the curry and rice she cooked in hostel kitchens. Priyanka is prone to start laughing and be unable to stop, and her friends set her giggles as ring tones. She loves baking bread, wearing saris, sleeping, and dreaming in Spanish. She is currently in Bangalore, the southern Indian city of gardens and lakes, planning her next adventure to Morocco. Subscribe to Priyanka's window onto the world at www.onmycanvas.com.

Crossing

Emily Wheeler

This story is not to be mistaken for a modern-day version of Chaucer's *The Canterbury Tales*. You won't find revelations, tears, or epiphanies here. This is simply the border crossing of six strangers in a tan-colored *colectivo* bus that rattles disconcertingly as it passes through the Atacama Desert in northern Chile. It is the tale of six individuals who will never meet again, narrated by a foreign woman with limited Spanish skills.

Come on, then, if you want to hear this thing out. It begins with the passengers.

The driver is a Chilean national clad in a plaid button-up and a straw hat that hangs down over his forehead. He is chewing something, his right cheek rising up and falling down, and when he isn't at that, he hums a melody under his breath. The inside of the car's windshield houses a faded image of the Virgin Mary that he stuck there some years ago, streaks of light coming out from behind her head.

In the passenger seat is a small Peruvian man who is tapping his hand against the top of his thigh, again and again. He's clutching a can of Coca-Cola in his other hand, beads of sweat forming across his forehead.

There are three more travelers in the back seat. A dark-skinned Chilean woman in athletic clothing sits next to a fifty-something-year-old Colombian mother applying eyeliner. Her Colombian son sits on the far-left seat, twisting a metal ring in his nose. Between mother and son they are balancing a large, cardboard box on their legs that has been sealed up with layers of clear tape.

Our narrator is up front, the sixth passenger in this tiny vehicle. There's a makeshift seat in between the driver and passenger side, and that's where she's been placed, one leg stuck against the stick shift and the other brushing the long green shorts worn by the Peruvian.

The Peruvian is talking now to the driver, and he's saying, "I am going over the border to bring my children back to Chile."

The driver spits out of his open window. "Immigration is complicated," he responds.

The car is speeding along a single lane highway marked by dark-colored pavement. Everything else in sight is yellow sand, stretching as far as our narrator can see. She tilts her head to look out of the window through her thick, black glasses, watching as sand dune after sand dune is passed by – no houses, signs, nothing else to be seen.

"Chile is a country of extremes," the driver tells her.

She is still looking out at the desert when she asks, "Can you go camping out there?"

He laughs and answers, "There are thousands of landmines buried out there. It happened during our war with Peru."

She looks over at the Peruvian who is facing straight ahead, mouth closed. The wind coming through the window barely moves his hair and clothes.

The driver switches to English. "It's better that way, you know. If you make a man lose a leg, the government has to pay for his care. Gives them more trouble financially. If you just kill men, then wars will never end."

Ahead in the distance is a white building, undecorated except for a large Chilean flag hanging slack in the air. In the back, the Colombian mother is making small noises, every once in a while muttering, "*Dios mío.*" The driver is humming a song loudly now, and the Chilean woman in the back smiles. The

Peruvian holds his head in his hands.

The driver pulls over, parking at the side of the road.

"This is the border crossing," he announces, "Hurry through so we can make it to Tacna at a decent time."

There is a long line of people waiting to enter the immigration point, passports in hand. The five passengers get in line while the driver stands by the car, chewing something again behind his right cheek. The Colombian mother and son are holding five pieces of luggage and the big box between them, and the mother pants each time the line moves. Both the Chilean woman and Peruvian man have one small black bag apiece. Our narrator is carrying a large, worn-out camping backpack, one of the small pockets is ripped open on the side. When they reach the front of the line, the driver appears, and they all receive their stamps.

"Welcome to Peru," says the driver once they are back in the colectivo, driving down a new highway that is stained by sand. On the sides of the road there are shakily planted billboards advertising restaurants and hotels that no longer exist.

"If I convert this money into *soles*, what should I get?" our narrator asks the driver, holding out folded bills in her hand.

"Two hundred – and don't accept less," he instructs.

The landscape is slowly becoming greener. Small bushes appear on the sides of the highway. Soon they pass buildings with broken windows and palm trees rising from the sand.

The Colombian mother asks the Chilean woman why she is traveling to Peru. "I am looking for my father," she says, but she doesn't add more.

Crisscrossed roads signal the start of the city. The colectivo turns a few times, and passes a roundabout. The driver pulls off into a neighboring parking lot. Across the street there is a long brick building with buses lined up outside. The passengers take out their money and pass their fares to the driver. One by one they leave, heading towards the bus station, waving goodbye to the remaining travelers behind.

Our narrator is the last to go, crawling out of the front seat and stretching to touch her toes. The driver has left the car, too, and he takes her luggage from the trunk. He holds her bag while she straps it to her back.

"Good luck out there," he says, his straw hat casting a shadow across his face, "And where are you headed, anyway?" He lights up a cigarette, the smoke drifting off in a cloud behind him.

"North, I guess," she answers, pulling a map out of her backpack.

"North," he repeats, taking another drag on his cigarette. For a moment they stand there in silence, their shadows running parallel to one another, the gravel of the parking lot adding textures to their black reflections. In the distance she can see tall hills of sand with winding roads going up, a few buses and cars driving around the curves until she can't see them anymore.

"North," he says again, nodding his head, while she walks toward the bus station.

Emily Wheeler

Emily is from Washington D.C., USA, and has filled her passport and gathered her stories by living in Germany, South Korea, and Colombia. She is a short story writer with a Bachelor's degree in English Writing and German Language from Hope College, and the recipient of the Distinguished Artist Award in writing from her alma mater. She lives in Bogota, Colombia, where she works as a first grade teacher and writes about her experiences in South America. Updates on her work can be followed at www.emilykwheeler. wixsite.com/authorpage.

The Clash

Susan Walsh

I finally realised my lifelong ambition to visit Chile at the age of fifty-eight, when I decided to retire from my stressful job, pack up my belongings and move to Santiago for a year. I don't particularly like the term retired as it implies a disengagement and prefer the Spanish word *jubilada*, which more aptly describes my renewed energy for the next stage of my life.

My plan was to explore South America, but I also wanted to participate in local and community life and experience a different culture first-hand. I told people I wanted to have *una aventura* (an adventure) but with some stability and familiarity of surroundings – and preferably with access to my own toilet. I later learned *una aventura* can also mean a love affair, which seemed to encapsulate an even greater sense of possibility and excitement.

As an older solo traveller, people's reactions have been mixed, ranging from high praise to puzzlement and concern. Although I accept I may not be the average traveller, I do wonder whether my actions would have received the same scrutiny if I had been younger.

With the farewell messages of friends and family still reverberating in my head, I arrived at Santiago airport and navigated the excellent metro system carrying a huge suitcase and two rucksacks. I finally emerged into the blinding September sunshine in Santiago's commercial centre, Sanhatton. With anonymous high-rise glass-fronted buildings and North American fast food outlets on every corner, it wasn't the culture shock I had been expecting. I had researched different neighbourhoods before embarking on the trip and knew that this was one of the safest for travellers. I still held on tightly to my bags, hyper aware of everyone around me, while I enjoyed my first coffee and an avocado sandwich.

Why did I choose Chile? One reason was to learn Spanish, which I thought would be a doddle after seven years spent completing a doctorate. I soon discovered (and all Chileans agree) that Chile has its own version of Spanish with a particular vocabulary, including a great deal of slang. Not only that, but speakers skip certain consonants, and even some of the vowels. Chileans speak quickly too. When I took a trip to the Uyuni salt flats later, our Bolivian guide didn't speak as quickly as most Chileans, even after consuming a bag of stimulating coca leaves to help with the high altitude.

I enrolled in a language school for the first two months and moved in with a wonderful host family. The school had assured me that I would not be the only older person taking classes. They were wrong. I was the oldest by thirty years. Despite the age difference, my classmates, who were mostly backpacking around South America, were very welcoming and tolerant of my slow progress in Spanish. The teachers were also excellent, but because of the demographics, conversation practice usually centred on the previous night's drunken and sexual exploits. While I have plenty of experience in the aforementioned activities, as an older person I couldn't help feeling a little uncomfortable sharing them in that setting. Discomfort turned to outrage when one tutor told me that he didn't know how to include me in discussions since I didn't have a boyfriend or husband (and by his tone clearly had no chance of getting one).

We were able to put our differences aside when the same tutor revealed that his favourite band was The Clash (a UK punk band from my generation), and we achieved lasting rapport when we performed a raunchy duet of "Rock the Casbah" in front of a bemused class of students who were not even born when The Clash were ripping it up.

When it came to exploring the country, my age didn't seem

to matter. However, I did face several unfounded assumptions at times, such as the idea that I wouldn't understand technology when, in fact, I used to teach it. Or that I was not aware of my personal safety. I was acutely aware of my conspicuousness as a *gringa*. I hardly ever left home without a money belt, or storing my valuables somewhere on my person, and I never experienced any problems. A further advantage of being older was that I had the confidence to say no when situations appeared unsafe, and I was less inclined to be out drunk in potentially dangerous situations.

Living with a host family was a brilliant introduction to Chilean food, music and dance. One disadvantage of being older was that I am perhaps a little more set in my ways. I was used to my own minimalist apartment in the UK and unprepared for the number of trinkets crammed into every corner of my new abode. It didn't matter as my host's warm welcome made me feel immediately at home. She was passionate about tango dancing and on many an afternoon we would roll back the carpet, turn on the music and practice our steps. On Sunday afternoons, she would also invite me to meet other tango enthusiasts in a dance hall above the local fire station.

These dance sessions begin with *onces* – an afternoon tea consisting of tea or coffee, sandwiches and cake – which is probably not the best preparation for cutting shapes on the dance floor immediately afterwards. The women are then obliged to wait to be asked to dance, and when asked, they are obliged to say yes. This provided me with an interesting insight into gender politics.

To become more familiar with local culture, I travelled on public transport, shopped at the market and went running in the park. I joined a patchwork course, a trekking group, and a film society. I socialised with friends over many a pisco sour or a bottle of good wine.

During my stay, I realised that this is a continent where natural disasters – as well as the threat of economic instability and political unrest – pose a much bigger risk than attacks on person or property.

Earthquakes, fires and landslides occur on a daily basis. I first experienced an earthquake one Friday at my language school. It seemed mildly exciting until months later, when we'd had fifty-eight such quakes in a week, eight of those in the space of an hour. By then, home was a ninth floor flat downtown and it felt like I was living in a washing machine.

The devastating forest fires that hit parts of south and central Chile in early 2017 were perhaps the worst the country has ever faced. While there was a touching collective response, the fires were a reminder – if one was needed – of the huge human, economic and environmental toll.

As I immersed myself in all aspects of Chilean life, I was conscious of echoes of Chile's history, and the complications of its present. I am old enough to remember the dictatorship years of Augusto Pinochet. At that time I was experiencing my own political awakening as I realised there was a world beyond the personal freedoms I enjoyed in my comfortable suburban life in the UK. How do people recover from such a systematic assault on personal identity and collective consciousness?

The images of tanks and troops on the streets of Santiago are forever etched on my memory. Those images became even more real to me when I accompanied a Chilean friend to the Museum of Memory and Human Rights, dedicated to commemorating the victims of the Pinochet years. Until then, she had not been able to face this terrible period of her country's history. Tears streamed down her face as we walked around, viewing the testimonies in silence.

I also remembered Sting's protest song "They Dance Alone (Cueca Solo)." He wrote it in 1987 after he saw a news story about Chilean women moving alone to their national dance, the Cueca. They had pictures of husbands, fathers,

brothers, or sons who had disappeared either held as dance partners or pinned to their clothes. During my stay I learned that the Cueca is a re-enactment of a courting ritual, making the absence of the male partner even more poignant.

Writer Isabel Allende's blend of political and social insights, magical storytelling and evocative descriptions of Chilean culture, set in glorious and diverse landscapes, ignited my interest in this complex country. The divisive class system she describes was immediately evident in downtown Santiago (where I eventually decided to live), a million miles from those high-rise buildings in the part of town known as Sanhatton.

She also writes about the resilience of people who will make and sell anything to get by. I regularly bought food from street vendors and it was always delicious, cheap, and posed no threat to my health. As a solo woman navigating this new country, I wanted to connect with all walks of life so I could understand how the country worked. That local knowledge was important in terms of my personal safety, but even more important were the wonderful connections I made with people who showed me how Chileans think, behave, and feel.

I have understood that perceived threats from others need to be understood within the context of the effects of poverty, denial of human rights and deep divisions in society. However, if you seek out the human qualities of care, support and community, you will find they exist in abundance. Being solo has allowed me to live more closely to local people, to make friends and learn how different cultural systems work. Not only did I feel less vulnerable, it enriched my whole Chilean experience.

Susan Walsh

Susan is a former health care professional and university lecturer from the UK. She lived in Santiago, Chile, for one year, pursuing her passion for exploring other cultures and learning languages. Susan has backpacked throughout Europe, Asia, Africa, and Central America, but wanted to experience a form of travelling that didn't mean living out of a rucksack. In Santiago, she built on her previous interests in health and social care through volunteering in various community-based projects. She also explored the rest of Chile and parts of Argentina, Bolivia, and Peru. Susan is passionate about women her age travelling solo in Latin America and is keen to dispel the myth that women face more dangers in this region than they do anywhere else in the world.

Incoherent in Copacabana

Camille Mansell

I stood on the swirly black and white mosaic pavement waiting to cross the esplanade along Copacabana Beach in Rio de Janeiro when everything around me suddenly turned to darkness. I reached around blindly for something to hold and stared dumbly into the blackness that had swallowed me up. Confused, unsure what to do next and on the verge of panicking, I extended my foot, loosened my grasp on the pole and stepped off the pavement.

I had just arrived in Brazil for the beginning of a year-long round-the-world trip. In the taxi coming from Rio's airport, I had looked out the window with my heart full of wonder and excitement at the thought of discovering new sights, tastes and experiences during this long-awaited adventure.

A few years earlier, while at university, I'd picked Brazil for an assignment on international marketing. The only thing that had stuck with me from my research was how a Brazilian bikini is two to three inches smaller everywhere than a normal bikini. In the taxi I reflected that at the time, I had never thought I would get to visit Brazil.

When you're in Rio, the first thing you want to do is head to the beach. So after pulling my frumpy bikini out of my backpack, I put my Havaianas on and walked to Copacabana Beach. It was late January, so it was hot and the beach was packed with deeply tanned Brazilians. Even though I was coming from summer in Australia, I felt positively pasty as I spread my sarong on a small patch of sand.

At the hostel they had warned me of thieves operating along the beach and advised me not to take any valuables. Their warning hadn't outweighed my desire to capture my first outing in Brazil, so I had packed my new digital camera in my bag. I also carried more money than was wise, because I had no idea how much things cost and how much I might need.

Pressing my bag close to my side, I leaned back on my sarong and took in my surroundings. Rowdy Brazilians shouted and laughed while standing around the bit of sand they had claimed. Sunbathing women did little but switch sides to get an even tan and regularly apply a surprising number of creams and hair products. Off to one side people played beach volleyball and further ahead people stood in the water or kicked at the shallows.

Here I was, in Brazil, on Copacabana Beach. After a year of solid saving, frugal living and extensive research I was finally here and it was all so exciting. I wanted to commit this moment to memory, the sounds and activity of the people all about me. I wanted it to remind me to enjoy my freedom and make the most of every day of my travels.

After about half an hour lying about people-watching and getting increasingly sweaty, I needed to find something to slake my thirst. I gently shook the sand off my sarong and put on my skirt and flip-flops and started to weave my way back across the beach. The sand was burning through the soles of my flip-flops and I began to feel a bit woozy. Now I definitely knew I needed water.

I got to a little kiosk with a thatched roof by the road and asked the attendant *"Tem agua?"* Unbelievably, they didn't have any water, or at least that's what I understood. I decided to cross the esplanade and walk towards the hostel. I was bound to find a little shop or supermarket on the way.

That's when I stepped out into the traffic, blinded.

As my foot left the kerb, a man broke through the blackness and came towards me, grabbing my wrist. He had bleached blonde hair, and I couldn't understand what he was saying. He pulled me aside, sat me down on the pavement, and leaned me up against a pole. When I looked up, a woman was saying something to me. All I could reply was "*Agua, agua.*"

My head lolled back and my legs were slack in front of me. I couldn't move or think and was at the mercy of these two people. The woman returned and squatted in front of me, splashing me with water from a bucket used to make sandcastles. She then held a bottle of cold water to my lips.

As I started to revive and feel more coherent, I understood that the woman was speaking to me in English. She waved towards the guy with the bleached blonde hair who was hanging off a little bit, surveying the scene. He wanted to know if I was okay and if I needed him to accompany me anywhere. I looked over and tried to say a thousand thanks with my smile, and said that I would be okay, I just needed to rest a little. The woman relayed this message to him in Portuguese and he reluctantly continued on his way to whatever he had been doing before he rescued a stricken foreigner who clearly didn't have her wits about her.

The woman stayed with me for a little longer to make sure I really was okay and could stand on my own. Then she gathered her children, who had been watching from the periphery, and took her leave. I thanked her profusely, although it has never felt like enough, for having helped me with so much kindness at a moment when I was vulnerable.

On my way back to the hostel I stopped at a supermarket to buy electrolyte drinks and four litres of water. I wasn't going to be so unprepared again. Ahead of me I still had twelve more months of travelling alone.

Camille Mansell

Camille is from Mildura, Australia. She first came to South America in 2004 for a six-month trip, but travelled so slowly it took her eleven months. Camille returned to Latin America seven years after that first trip. She met her handsome prince, Edwin, after kissing a frog-shaped rock during the hike to Ciudad Perdida in Colombia, which inspired the story that was published in the *Was Gabo an Irishman?* anthology. Camille lives with Edwin and their son Daniel in Bogota, Colombia, and continues to travel across the region. Read more of her writing at www.alittlecameo.com.

Sweet Talkers

Nadia Ho de Guillén

It was February when I landed in Argentina, and the first thing I did when I entered Ezeiza International Airport was to get rid of the thick coat I was wearing before I roasted from the inside. The weather contrast from Prague in winter to Buenos Aires in summer couldn't have been sharper.

The next thing for me to work out was how to cope with Argentine Spanish. I had been studying Spanish for three semesters before the trip, but I was still shocked when I couldn't even understand people's directions to get to my new home. Argentine Spanish and the local *porteño* accent were so different from the language I had been taught at school that I found it extremely difficult to communicate.

I rented a room in an apartment near my university and shared it with an elderly Argentinian woman because I wanted to experience true Argentine life. Unfortunately, we got off to a bad start when I arrived home with a Japanese boy I had met at the airport. The landlady wasn't at all happy and refused to let him in. She taught me my first lesson in the country: Don't trust a person you have just met.

Communicating with the locals didn't get any better in the following days. While exploring the endless charm of the new city, I felt frustrated by my inability to connect, especially as the people seemed to be equally charming. I decided to enroll in a local language school for a three-week intensive Spanish course before commencing the new semester. One of my classmates was best friends with the U.S. singer Skylar Grey who sang the then-popular song, "Coming Home." I didn't know at the time how much those two words would come to mean to me. I'm coming home… to Vietnam, to the Czech Republic, to France, to Mexico, to Canada, to the USA. Being in Argentina was the start of countless journeys, and I would go on to make homes in numerous countries.

That six-month trip to Buenos Aires was my first long, solo journey. I was a twenty-one year-old student majoring in International Business at the University of Economics in Prague. It's fair to say that I was very young, very inexperienced and very innocent.

I hadn't had many opportunities to travel outside the Czech Republic, where I had permanent residence, before that, primarily because of my Vietnamese passport. Visa application processes can be a nightmare for those who have passports from developing countries. Hence my travel bug lay dormant for a long time, hopelessly wishing it could spread its wings and see the places it had learned about in textbooks. I had very little knowledge about Latin America except for the information I had gained in geography classes, which focused on the drug cartels, kidnappings, robberies, and other problems that the region was facing.

Nevertheless, an invisible charm attracted me to this unknown continent and I was determined to explore it, despite the concerns of my family and friends who kept asking, "How will you stay safe while traveling alone as a woman there?" Maybe their fear originated from the common belief that Latin America didn't favor women. Ultimately, this is where the word "macho" originated. I did not know the answer to their question, but for some reason, the more they opposed my going to the Southern hemisphere, the more I was attracted to traveling there.

I grew up as part of the so-called banana generation. It is a nickname given to kids who have parents from Asia, but grew up in Western countries and behave and think differently from "typical Asian people." I had a very strict upbringing and was expected to obey older members of my family. Also, it was not an option, but rather an obligation, to be the best in everything I did.

I was not allowed to have a boyfriend until I had finished my university education. This wasn't a difficult rule for me to follow because I enjoyed spending my leisure time studying and writing diaries. Instead of having a boyfriend, I preferred to date my books and succeed academically. Besides, I considered myself too ugly for Czech boys. I was definitely not confident in myself and I felt lost between the two contrasting cultures.

Argentina flipped my self-image one hundred and eighty degrees. Any foreign woman who has visited the country will know how passionate and flirty Argentinian men can be. The way the men spoke to me made me feel attractive and self-confident in a completely new way. They can get your head whirling around like a fidget spinner. Ah, those *chamuyeros* (sweet talkers). They would do anything for just one kiss. When they needed or wanted a woman, they sure knew how to get her.

I had experienced my own dose of Argentine charm back in the Czech Republic with a handsome, blond Argentinian boy who was on an exchange program at my home university. The fling continued for a semester, and before I knew it, I had fallen in love with him. Sadly, he felt otherwise and was actually dating a Brazilian woman living in London at the same time he was with me. Ah, those chamuyeros. He broke contact when he knew I wanted our relationship to get serious, but we met again as lovers and then as friends in Buenos Aires.

As my self-confidence grew, I faced some big challenges academically. At the start of the semester I discovered that most of my courses in English had been cancelled and I would have to take them in Spanish instead. I felt hopeless since I believed that I would never be able to pass the exams with my mediocre Spanish. But I had no choice. Subjects like Public Relations were particularly hard, since some professors

expected me to speak perfect Spanish prior to enrolling in their classes. I failed that mid-term exam, but it didn't discourage me, instead it made me determined to study even harder in order to succeed. Inspired by W. E. B. Du Bois' line that "There is no force equal to a woman determined to rise," I passed all the classes with good grades.

Immersing myself in the local culture between classes brought lots of positive surprises. Everywhere, locals drank burning hot *mate* from calabash gourds through metal straws, even on the beach under the scorching heat of the sun. In the classroom, students and teacher alike would share the same gourd – sharing is definitely caring in *mate* drinking culture.

In the evenings, I attended tango dancing classes at the tango houses and admired couples of all ages dancing so passionately, without caring if they made mistakes. This was a huge difference between the European/Asian and Latin American cultures. Instead of being afraid of losing face, Latin Americans enjoy themselves without worrying about what other people think of them. It was a big lesson for me. You may be young or old, slim or overweight, a success or a failure, but whatever your flaws are, if you treat yourself well and are satisfied with what you have, others will eventually respect you.

During my six-month stay in Argentina I traveled to the carnival in Gualeguaychú, to the wine region of Mendoza, and to Che Guevara's birthplace, Rosario, with friends from all corners of the world. We still keep in touch, and I can honestly say that I made some of the best relationships in my life there.

I grew up being a rather timid person, but I found a new sense of adventure in Latin America and dared to go paragliding, white water rafting, and rappelling in the Andes. The region helped me get out of my comfort zone, and through these adventurous and risky activities my new ideology emerged: You only live once, so enjoy every moment of it. As an old Argentine proverb says, "A man who develops himself is born twice." If we are stuck in one place or one situation for too long and are hesitant to move forward, we'll allow life to pass us by.

I returned to the Czech Republic a new person: I was much more positive, friendly, and open-minded. I believe that we cannot choose where we are born, but we can choose where we leave our hearts. For me, that place is Latin America.

It may not surprise you to hear that a year later I fell in love with a Latin American man who then became my husband. But that love story I'll tell another time.

Nadia Ho de Guillén

Nadia grew up in Vietnam and the Czech Republic, and has also lived, studied and worked in Argentina, Canada, Mexico and France. She currently resides in the USA with her Mexican husband. Nadia holds a Bachelor's degree in International Business from the University of Economics in Prague, Czech Republic, and a Master's degree in International Brand Management from Kedge Business School, Marseille, France. Her wide professional scope ranges from international business, academic research, and consulting to marketing, event management, and cross-cultural communication. She has worked at nonprofit organizations, international corporations, universities, startups and global citizenship projects. Nadia is the author and co-author of three books published in Vietnam and will soon publish a book in English about female world travelers. Her website, *A Mile in Our Shoes*, collects personal stories of women from around the world at www.amileinourshoes.org.

Pointers

Ilona Tonnaer

The place where I was standing might have been a bus stop, but it was pretty good at hiding it. Around me there was nothing but a dirt road, some green hills, and an abandoned wooden cabin across the street – nothing that said "This is definitely a place where travellers stop to get on a bus."

But this had to be the place. I had been sent here by pointers and they'd never really sent me to the wrong place before.

Before I go any further, I should explain a bit more about what I call "pointers." I had traveled a bit already. And I had made the journey that brought me to this bus stop without a plan. Not intentionally, but I have found that plans are always subject to change. You make one – a really good one – and the next moment it's worthless because a better option has come to the table. One that suits you right now. One that points you in a certain direction, which might even be the opposite of where you were planning to go.

At that moment, only one rule counts: always follow the pointers. It may not seem so at the time, but they will always send you the right way.

That's why I didn't have the slightest doubt that right now, this was the place I needed to be. Here in the sun with my ridiculously large backpack, by the side of a dirt road in what you may very well call the middle of nowhere. It wouldn't be the first time after all …

"Hey!"

Startled by the sudden human sound, I tried to look over my shoulder. It wasn't easy because of the aforementioned ridiculously large backpack on my shoulders. Was that the old man that just biked by, yelling at me from a distance? He had looked surprised when he saw me standing here, and I even thought for a second he was going to wave at me. I actually thought about waving at him. But was he calling me now?

"Hey, *gringa*!"

Yes. Definitely calling me. That's me. The gringa. Anywhere I go. Blond hair, light eyes, fragile frame. That's a gringa. It didn't surprise me that that he called me a gringa. What surprised me was that this man of a certain age who'd cycled past had now turned around and was calling me. Alarm bells were ringing. What does he want? Who was this guy? Why was he cycling around this forgotten old land? The storm of alarming thoughts died down as he slowly approached. He couldn't have looked any friendlier and – trusting my developed instincts and good character judgement (ever since the day gypsies "borrowed" all my cash) – I decided I could trust him.

He stopped right in front of me and stepped off his bike, smiling his wide South American smile. "Hey gringa. I saw you standing here and I thought, what is that girl doing out here, all alone? Are you a tourist? On your way somewhere? Do your parents know you're here?"

Just to be clear: these are the kind of questions I get all the time. Especially the latter. Especially from older people. They usually ask how old I am next.

"How old are you, traveling here all by yourself?"

I put on my loveliest smile, the one that is designed for these moments and these questions. I'm Dutch. Nineteen years-old. And yes, my parents know I'm here. No, they're probably not getting any sleep. But that is correct, they did allow me to visit this corner of the world, all alone. Or the center of the world, depending on your point of view. No, he doesn't have to worry. And yes, I am on my way somewhere. Petrohué. Because this is a bus stop, I add firmly.

"A bus stop? Here? Never knew there was one. And I live nearby. But alright, if you say so. Petrohué, you said? Great place. Should do that for sure. But hey, you know what? My son is a tour guide. Really nice guy, born and raised here, he can show you everything. I am sure he will take you there. That way you won't have to wait for the bus. His office is really close," he said, pointing to the other side of the road. Ah, so the wooden cabin I'd been looking at all this time across the road was not abandoned, at all. It is an office, for Pete's sake. An office that helps travelers go to Petrohué. Why am I not surprised? Hello, pointer.

I came to this continent because of a pointer. A girl told me she had visited Argentina and loved it, so I figured I'd go there. For those of you paying attention right now: you are right, Petrohué is not in Argentina. It's in Chile. That's because when I got to Argentina, I followed some more pointers that brought me here. There was a woman, who braided hair in the street, called Maria who told me that Chile was Argentina plus. "Why hang around in Bariloche when you can just as easily cross the border?" she asked. There was no arguing with that. So I crossed the border. And I don't regret it.

Another pointer was a man I talked to in the supermarket line. I have forgotten his name, let's call him… Peter. I forgot the town's name too. But there I was, in line. Peter too.

"While you are here," he said, "You have to go to Petrohué. Believe me, you won't regret it. It is paradise on earth. Blue lagoons, green woods, and the Osorno volcano painted in the background…"

"You had me at blue lagoons," I told him.

That's how pointers work.

A pointer doesn't have to be a Peter or Maria. It can also be me. And some are anti-pointers. Like when I fell asleep on the bus to Petrohué and woke up a long way away in Puerto Montt.

Puerto Montt may have been a pointer, but only to ensure I appreciated the rest of Chile. It was a sad place with a chilly, silent vibe. Freaky. Like I'd landed in a Tim Burton movie.

I found a hotel which appeared to be little more than an abandoned hallway completely covered with red carpet. And not a soul to be seen. I followed the only stairs in the narrow hallway up to the first floor, where I found more red carpet and a lady who was remarkably old and skinny for this part of the world. Plus a dog, which was even skinnier and bonier than her lady boss.

The dog and the lady took me to my room. It had high ceilings and curtains that didn't stop blowing in the wind. Seriously, they didn't stop. It was as if they'd been deliberately programmed for a traveler-enters-creepy-looking-hotel-in-a-cold-abandoned-city scene. But it would have to do for the night.

That's all I saw of Puerto Montt. Oh, that and the money-borrowing gypsies, they were there too. Anti-pointers. Fine. It was good to see the less cool side of this otherwise awesome country. And I was on my way to the blue lagoons. The next day I took the bus and arrived in Osorno, Ensenada. I stood at a bus stop where I met an old man on a bicycle. Yes, that's where we were.

And there he was. The son who did tours to Petrohué, in his wooden cabin across the road. It's not just the landscapes that are beautiful in South America. What a guy. Hair black as the night, wildly curled, little Juanes beard underneath. I arrived in the cabin and knew right away that this was where all my pointers had been pointing.

The son took me to Petrohué, which indeed – just as Peter had promised – was a wonderful place, full of lagoons, green woods and a volcano view. He showed me the Chilean forest and named every plant and tree we saw. We found hidden lakes and talked about life and trees, we rode his motorbike up to a volcano and watched the sunset from there, and we looked for crabs on a volcanic beach. We collected all sorts of fruit in the forest and later made jelly with his grandmother, we climbed trees to watch the stars, we took naps on the black sand beach and had barbecues with his friends and family.

These pointers brought me more than a lagoon. This was the real Chile: nature, volcanoes, family, friends, food and adventure. We did whatever came to our minds. I figured that's how travelling on your own is done.

All those places and moments in this amazing region showed me that I was in exactly the right place. All those pointers. Like when I knocked at a stranger's door in the middle of the night looking for a hostel and was instantly taken in and offered the youngest daughter's princess bed.

Or when I met a fisherman who promised to take me fishing but then asked me to come back half an hour later because he hadn't finished his beloved *mate* (the drink, not the friend). I was welcome to join him in the meantime, he said. *Bebida* before business. I loved it.

And that one time when I visited what used to be a prison in Santiago and an ex-prisoner, Pedro, told me about his legendary escape from it in 1993. Fifteen inmates spent five months digging a hole from the private visitor's room for married couples to the sewers, he said, and crawled to freedom.

Then there were the Argentinian Bocas, who taught me what it means to be a real football supporter. Screaming at the coach, cheering my ass off. My dad would be so proud of me.

I would wake up in the night to look out of the window and see a bright full moon reflected on the lake in front of a volcano, only to close my eyes again and wonder if I was dreaming, or was I really in paradise on earth?'

And then there was my friend Deborah's grandpa. Deborah welcomed me to her house in Valparaíso and, just like with so many others, there was no question of treating me like a tourist. I was part of the family from the moment I set foot on the doorstep.

Families celebrate Easter together and it was "so sad" my mom had to celebrate Easter without me. I had my Easter eggs in Deborah's grandparent's bedroom. Because that's where her grandfather was. In bed. Terminally ill. He just didn't know that. They told me they thought it was best that way.

There I was. An almost-adopted, curious teenage tourist – without the backpack for the moment – with people who had invited me into their home to eat at their tables and to celebrate this special intimate moment as a family. Connected in sadness at this man's death bed.

He looked at me and he said he was happy I was there. He asked if I like South America and if it's prettier than where I come from. And yes, whether my mother knows I'm here. "Life is so short," he said with a soft, melancholic smile. "Enjoy it while you are young." Then I knew: he knew what he was not supposed to know. He knew that he was dying. This man, in his PJs in the soft afternoon light of his Valparaíso room full of Easter eggs; he was the most important pointer of them all. I know that now.

Ilona Tonnaer

Ilona, from the Netherlands, was a journalist, albeit unknowingly, even before she studied to be one. She wasn't the kind of journalist who yells at politicians, though, but the kind with a natural curiosity about people who likes to see and meet them in many different places. Ilona traveled South America for five months before she completed her journalism studies. She believes the region and its people made her the person she is today: a twenty-eight year-old naturally curious journalist and a writer who loves to read and write other people's stories, whether real or with a fantastical twist.

Change in Your Pocket

Andrea Jaramillo

I walked briskly down the street, catching the last of the evening light as it bathed the city in shades of purple and blue. The breeze was fresh on my face, like taking gulps of sweet water. I listened to the hum of the boulevard below me. The sounds of buses loading and unloading, honking, grinding, screeching. Far enough from the chaos, I observed these sounds. City sounds. My city's sounds. In that moment, despite the chaos, it all felt peaceful. Life was as sweet as the breeze that enveloped me.

I reached into the pocket of my vest and pulled out three coins. *Pesos.* I thought about how, just four months before, my nightstand held small piles of dimes and quarters, waiting to be used again back home. Circulated back into my old life. Or how the bottom of my purse always held a spare quarter amongst loose pesos. Where did those quarters and dimes go? When did this change occur?

This must be what it feels like to call someplace home; when the change in your pocket no longer seems foreign. When your dollars are replaced with pesos and you understand the weight of them in your hand.

When I made it to the end of the block, I saw the road in front of me, bustling with rush hour commuters, and put the coins back in my pocket. Perhaps diving into the unknown in life is not always as abrupt as one might expect. I went on this adventure alone, knowing exactly who and what I would be leaving behind, but feeling ready for this new unknown, my new home. The change felt gradual. Difficult at times, stretching me from side to side in ways I didn't know were possible, but all the while shaping me into the new person I am supposed to be. Maybe becoming accustomed to your new life and your new home is as gradual as the change in your pocket. My thoughts hovered above me, intertwining with smog and soot from the street, mingling until they diluted each other.

I was at a crossroads. I had walked down my quiet, tree-lined street as safe and comfortable as my old life had been until I was met with the chaos of this boulevard's intersection. Fast, ever-changing, and uncertain: this new life of mine. The intersection of old and new, of safe and unknown. I should turn back and go home, relax after a long day, I thought. I turned onto the boulevard and kept walking into the sunset.

Andrea Jaramillo

Andrea is a cultural researcher from Los Angeles, USA, who packed two suitcases and moved to Bogota, Colombia, for two years so she could explore her roots and spend time with her extended family. She fell in love with the country, its people, and their culture. Following this first big move she has lived in Barcelona, Spain, and New York City, USA, where she has continued her discoveries and her writing. A lover of cultural experiences, good food, and a great book, Andrea shares her tales of the people and places she encounters on her blog, *Andre Abroad*. She currently lives between Bogota and Los Angeles. Check out www.andreabroad.com and follow Andrea on Instagram: @andreabroadblog.

The Island of Dead Dolls

Fayida Jailler

Arriving at the Floating Gardens in Xochimilco is an assault on the senses. Groups of men clamour and holler, competing to encourage the crowds to climb aboard their own brightly coloured boat. Mariachis play along the water and the smell of gasoline mixes with the aroma of food that floats across the canal. In the midst of everything are the tourists, milling around and trying to make sense of it all.

The wooden boats are called *trajineras*. They are long and narrow punts, hand-painted in vibrant mixtures of pink, yellow, red, green and blue. Each boat carries a table and two benches covered by an ornate canopy, and each has its name displayed on a wooden board out front. Many of the boats are named after women: Esperanza, Lupita, Mariana, Isabella, Ximena and Teresa. I search for my own name among the trajineras parked along the bank but, of course, I don't see it. There is a boat moored a short walk away with the name Xochimilco painted on its board in white, capital letters. That will have to do.

The punter is a young man called Rogelio. He is smiley and warm as I climb on board alongside a handful of other excited tourists.

We set off down the canal. Rogelio is perched at the head of the boat with a long wooden pole, and he pushes us forward with strong strokes as we glide through the water. The canal is flanked by trees, the water laps against the banks and the sun is strong as it beats down upon our boat.

Rogelio tells me the plots of land that line the bank are

chinampas, a Mesoamerican agricultural system, and I soon realise that a whole community inhabits the Floating Gardens. This is not just a tourist attraction, it's home to every person who lives along its waterways, an entire society built on a labyrinth of canals. They punt up and down the waterway as you and I would walk along a street. And like a street there is traffic; we navigate the lanes and compete with the neighbouring trajineras that try to pass us.

People hire the boats for celebrations, too. On one boat a full mariachi band, dressed in pristine white suits and large brimmed hats, serenades a family. The guests share food and conversation, smiles and laughter. One woman holds a Chihuahua wearing a frilly blue dress. The atmosphere is raucous and joyful, and the revellers salute us as we pass.

Rogelio asks if anyone is hungry and he calls to a boat a few yards ahead. We pull up alongside it. A woman stands in the centre, surrounded by pots and plates in her very own floating kitchen.

"What do you want?" Rogelio asks. "She's got *quesadillas, tacos, pambazos, tlacoyos de maza azul…*"

Feeling adventurous, I opt for a *tlacoyo* and am presented with a delicious mass of cooked dark blue dough with chopped cactus and cheese on top. As we continue down the canal we see a man on the bank, playing a guitar. I close my eyes and bask in the heat, the sounds, and the scents as the melody washes over me. I feel like a different person, removed from the life I left behind. All the faces, memories, responsibilities, obligations… for a moment, I let them go. They stretch out behind me like the ripples that form behind our boat as Rogelio pushes us forward.

The presence of the other trajineras soon begins to fade and I realise the waterways have become congested with plants instead. We hear nothing but the sound of the water and the occasional call of a bird.

I look up and see a baby's body, hanging from a tree.

My heart jumps.

"It's okay, it's okay," Rogelio says. "It's just a doll. They're all dolls. Look."

Countless pairs of soulless, plastic eyes stare back at me. There are thousands of dolls, hanging lifeless from every tree. They are filthy and deformed with severed limbs, decapitated heads, encrusted features, matted hair, plastic grins and those dead, staring eyes. I watch them swaying in the breeze. It looks like Hell on earth.

"What is this place?"

"The Island of Dolls," Rogelio says.

Rogelio draws the boat closer to the island. The hairs on my arms stand up as we approach. The dolls greet us in silence with their unwavering, demented smiles.

I feel nervous as we climb ashore. There are dolls everywhere; strapped to trees, to the fence lining the water's edge, to the rusted barbed-wire fixtures that hang like clothing lines. At my feet lie piles of withering orange flower petals. It is *cempasúchitl*, marigolds, the Mexican flower of death.

Ahead is a cabin, which has yet more dolls strapped to its filthy, wooden slats. I move closer and see that their features are caked with cobwebs.

"Can I go in?" I ask the caretaker.

The cabin is spacious and filled with light. Dust shimmers in the sun beams. It's empty apart from the dolls suspended from the ceiling and the wooden pillars that support the roof, and I feel the dolls watching me as I venture inside. On one wall is a shrine surrounded by flowers and trinkets and a bowl of coins, playing cards, and bracelets that have been left in honour of the deceased.

In the centre sits a large, finely dressed doll. She is the Queen of this island and she gazes in silence upon her macabre little empire.

"That's Augustinita," the caretaker says, "His favourite. The first doll he found."

"Whose favourite?" I ask, "Who did this?"

He points to a yellowing photograph of an old man, pinned to the wall above the doll and says in a slow, deliberate voice:

"Julian Santana Barrera."

The ground squelched beneath his feet as Don Julian stepped outside his cabin. It had rained throughout the night but the island was at its best at dawn, when the sun bathed everything in its calm, blue glow.

Don Julian set off on his usual route with Lucho, who bounded ahead, disappearing into the rushes only to emerge further along the bank. The canal had risen from the rainfall and the air felt cleaner, as if both had been purged of the heat and the stress of the previous day.

It was Lucho who found her. The dog barked wildly, rushed out of the undergrowth and ran in frenzied circles around Don Julian's feet.

"What is it?" he said, "Lucho, calm down!"

Lucho whined and whimpered. Don Julian ran towards the rushes and saw a small foot protruding from the grass. He stepped closer, his heart hammering in his chest. It was a little girl in a white dress, lying face down in the water beside the bank. Her black hair bobbed gently with the tide. Her dress was stained with mud. She looked as if she had flailed and struggled until the last moment of her life.

Don Julian was afraid to touch the child but he knew he couldn't leave her there. He gripped the cold skin of her shoulder and rolled her onto her back. Her lifeless eyes stared at him, her cheeks were pale and her blue lips were slightly parted. Don Julian stumbled backwards and fell, breathing heavily. What was a child doing alone by the river? He leaned forward, clutched his head and cried.

The death was ruled an accident. In the days that followed, the community gathered together to bury the girl.

They placed flowers and candles by the spot where Don Julian had found the child, along with orange *cempasúchitl* petals, rice, and small heaps of salt to cleanse and guide her soul on its way to the afterlife.

On the night of the funeral, Don Julian sensed he was not alone. An unknown presence seemed to linger in the corner of his cabin. He felt it in the flicker of the lights and the creak of the door in the breeze. Even Lucho seemed subdued, curled up in a corner of the cabin.

Don Julian tried to sleep, but every time he closed his eyes he saw the girl's glassy eyes staring at him. He imagined he could feel her dripping hair as she leaned over him, and the clammy feel of her hand as she touched his face. He sat up, feeling tense and heard a sound outside his window. It sounded like a muffled sob.

Don Julian pulled on his shoes and scrambled for his oil lamp. He raced outside, with Lucho at his feet. He was convinced he could hear the sound of a child crying in the darkness, but he could see no one there.

He made his way through the black sludge towards the bank until he reached the spot where he had found the girl. The crying became louder and louder, until it was joined by the sound of Don Julian's own sobs.

"I'm so sorry," he choked into the night. "I'm so, so sorry."

It seemed so natural when he found the doll, abandoned in the reeds. She was missing a foot and her clothes were covered in mud, but he was fascinated by her symmetrical features and her pretty, auburn ringlets.

"Augustinita," he whispered. He knew what he had to do.

He hung Augustinita from the tree outside his cabin, where he knew the little girl's spirit would find it. It wasn't long before he came across another doll, nestled in the foliage. She was missing an arm but he hung her beside Augustinita.

Don Julian continued with his ritual for years until dolls hung like fruit from every tree on his island. Each one was an offering to a lost, infant soul.

"People said he was obsessed," the caretaker said, gesturing towards the photo. "He wouldn't stop hanging dolls for the little girl. It became his life's work. People began coming to the island to see them and they started bringing their own dolls to leave at the shrine. Sometimes people tried to steal them, as souvenirs to show their friends, but bad things happened to those people. These dolls are cursed. They can never leave the island."

"What happened to *señor* Santana Barrera?"

"He died. They found his body in the very same spot where he found the little girl."

Time is running out on our tour of Xochimilco and Rogelio is keen to take us back to port. I climb aboard the trajinera and take a seat as he pushes away from the bank.

"What did you think?" he asks, grinning.

"I don't know," I say. "It's creepy and tragic but, in a way, it's beautiful."

"Some say they're possessed," Rogelio says. "They say the dolls move, sometimes they wave or turn their heads. My uncle swears they spoke to him once."

"Do you believe that?"

Rogelio shrugs.

"Sometimes I wonder if there are spirits among us, out on the water."

I look back at the island as we glide away. As the dolls' faces begin to diminish, I'm convinced I can hear the sound of a little girl crying.

Fayida Jailler

Fayida was born in South London, England, to a British mother and a Congolese father and has always been interested in foreign cultures. She studied French and Spanish at university and spent her year abroad in Mexico, where she fell in love with Latin America. She has since travelled alone to Cuba, Colombia, Puerto Rico, and the Dominican Republic. For Fayida, solo travel is as much a process of self-discovery as it is about cultural learning, because in the words of Les Brown, "In order to do something that you've never done, you have to become someone you've never been." Fayida works as a freelance journalist and documentary researcher. You can find her on Twitter at @fayidajailler, Instagram at fayida.jailler and through her website: www.fayidajailler.com.

But You're a Girl

Megan Benay

"But…you're a girl," the plump sweaty man in his twenties spluttered as he looked up at me from the bottom bunk of the crowded four-person room in Nicaragua.

Fact. I was a girl. I am a girl, or a woman I suppose, seeing as I'm a few years older now.

I smiled sweetly and set down my three hundred-pound bag. "Yes," I replied, "I am a girl and this is my room."

Two other men turned their heads towards me and muttered an indistinct "Hey" before rolling back over to continue sleeping off the night before. The room smelled like a pleasant combination of sweat disguised by Axe body spray and the distinct mildew-like aroma from the never-quite-dry "quick dry" towels that clings to many backpackers.

The plump man informed me that a guy had been sleeping in the room before me, and that I'd be the only girl in the room. A point he clearly thought needed highlighting, as if I had somehow missed this. He seemed a bit nervous as he tidied up some man-things strewn across the floor and offered me a corner to store my belongings.

This wasn't the first, or the last, time I would be flagged as the only lone-woman traveling Latin America in a sea of men. This lovely welcome does underscore, however, the continued rarity of finding a woman willing to "brave the dangers" and travel alone, especially south of the U.S. border.

I didn't start my solo Latin American adventures as some kind of feminist statement, and if I'm being honest, the fact that I was a single woman traveling abroad didn't factor into my planning at all, because I had done no planning and had no idea what to expect. I don't necessarily recommend this unprepared approach to travel, but I will say it allowed me to, at least initially, experience Latin America free from any of the 'it's dangerous, you'll probably get kidnapped and die' rhetoric that seems to accompany solo female traveling.

My travels began with a summer-long trip to Ecuador when I was twenty-five. Then came a vacation in Nicaragua and a move to Chile for four months before backpacking through many more countries. I never quite learned to plan my trips, but I did learn that the most formative and influential experiences of my life came from traveling alone as a woman in Latin America, and I wouldn't change it for anything.

Traveling alone, and in particular, traveling alone as a woman, is one of the greatest gifts you can give yourself. I understand the desire to travel as part of a crowd, to go on adventures with your bestie, and to have someone else to share your journey, but traveling on your own is an invaluable experience. Man or woman, the skills you gain from being on your own in a foreign country are those you can draw on for the rest of your life. Or so I assume. I am only twenty-eight.

Traveling alone, I learned how to rely on myself for company. And as my mother always reminded me when I was a sulky teenager full of angst, the greatest friend you will ever have is yourself, so you better learn to get along with her. When you travel alone, you discover your deepest values and convictions, and confront your fears of loneliness and isolation. You learn to be okay with being on your own, and rely on yourself to make decisions. There, I've said it: travel alone as a woman because it will teach you to love yourself and be your own best friend.

Traveling alone is a remarkable experience that everyone should undertake at some point in their life, and women travelers have no more to fear in Latin America than they do anywhere else.

Women, at least where I am from in the U.S., live in a modern era of female rights and equality while simultaneously cowering in fear of the unknown predator lurking in every dark corner. I am not a studied feminist, and I can't tell you why we women continue to perpetuate this dichotomy despite the societal progress we have made. What I can say is that the same measures you take to be smart, informed, and safe in your own country apply when you are traveling in Latin America, or anywhere else for that matter. Would you walk alone at night in an area you didn't know, without a way to call for help? Absolutely not, because you're an intelligent, modern woman who knows that it's not worth taking unnecessary risks. If this is the mentality you maintain in your own country, you need only to adopt the same mindset when traveling in Latin America.

If you are concerned that you will for some reason lose all sense of reason and fall prey to complete ineptitude while abroad, have no fear. You will be reminded time and time again that almost everything is dangerous, and you will get frustrated because you will believe you are only receiving these reminders because you are a woman. The reality is, those people may be making good points. Rather than taking their warnings as an offense, remember that these tales of caution come from a place of love. Not to mention that in times of actual danger you will be the wise lady who knows just what to do thanks to all the unsolicited but thoughtful advice you received from every man, woman and child along the way.

When I was traveling in Colombia, I arranged to meet up with my sweet but very young German friend with whom I had worked on a farm in Uruguay. He brought along his equally sweet and young friend, who was also male. Given their gender, I doubt they were regaled with nearly as many

tales of danger as I had been during their South American adventures. When they suggested we buy a few beers and drink them in a dark, deserted park rather than going to a well-lit and populated bar, my highly informed and cautioned female warning alarm began to blare.

"Hmm," I thought, "I wouldn't sit in a park at night in my own country, why would I do it abroad?" Not wanting to be a party-pooper, I agreed to sit with them. Five minutes later I watched as both German boys ran off in pursuit of the vagrants who had stolen their phones, and I felt grateful for the endless warnings I had received to keep my belongings safe and not engage with strangers. I walked over to the nearest police officer, showed him my hostel address on the map, asked him to walk me there, and took my wise, well-cautioned butt safely to bed.

This story could easily be told about any city in any country, and Latin America is not alone in having its share of dangers. As women, we have the benefit of understanding that the world is not always safe, but rather than feeling inhibited by fear we can feel empowered by cautious, smart thinking. Something my German friends apparently could have used too.

Traveling alone as a female in Latin America is also an opportunity to witness a set of gender norms that will help you realize the privileges many of us enjoy because of so many generations of women who fought for equality. This is not to say women in Latin American countries live antiquated, pre-suffrage-like versions of reality; there are any number of empowered, brilliant, independent and successful women in Latin America today.

But not all Latin American women have the rights and entitlements I expect and demand as a woman in my own society. I maintain a firm "nobody puts baby in a corner," mentality, which wasn't always well received. This was not only because my self-righteous attitude was perceived as rude but because it defied many traditional gender norms that I had not encountered in my somewhat sheltered life.

When I lived in Chile as a volunteer English teacher I was often confronted with these cultural differences in gender norms and they gave me a new perspective on the privileges I exercise daily without a second thought. When my host dad told me that I wasn't to go running because it was dangerous, I laughed and said I'd be fine – it was just a road after all, and "nobody puts baby in a corner." My refusal to adhere to his instruction was viewed as defiance and a further illustration of my arrogant U.S. nature. It took me weeks to return to his good graces. For the record, I was only able to return to them after insisting that I was trying not to become chubby, an argument that was considered valid for a woman. You can imagine how that made the ol' blood boil.

A close friend experienced a similar incident. She finally lost her temper with her elderly host father after he repeatedly said she was weak, even though she was in good shape and had never given him any reason to poke fun at her. Because she spoke her mind and said she felt hurt by his words, her host father refused to speak to her and she found herself stuck in an intolerable living situation. We seethed with anger and cursed a culture that allowed such blatant disrespect of women.

Time passed and relationships healed. We began to learn that what we had perceived as inconsiderate sexism was really just a difference in culture and gender norms. As guests of another country, we were not there to change mindsets or advocate the superiority of one culture over another. We were there to learn and experience a different way of life. What we had gained was a deep appreciation for the gender norms we take for granted in our own cultures, and a little more humility when it comes to understanding the privileges we exercise each day. The gender normative differences in Latin America are not something to be weary of, but something to learn and grow from.

When you travel in Latin America, you have the opportunity to get to know the remarkable women who live and travel throughout this region. From eighteen to eighty, these are some of the most interesting, unique, wise, insightful, and colorful women you will ever meet. I gained a sisterhood from all walks of life and they encouraged me to stretch the boundaries of what I ever thought was possible.

Women who travel alone in Latin America can do so in the knowledge that a plethora of inspiring women will be there by their sides as they conquer whatever comes next. So go forth, you strong, empowered women, and travel *solita amiga*.

Megan Benay

Megan is from Vermont, USA. After teaching special education in New York City for four years, she decided to hit the road and spent a summer in Quito, Ecuador. She fell in love with Latin America and, upon completing her M.Ed. in Organizational Leadership at Columbia University, moved to Chile to teach English with the United Nations Development Programme. After four spectacular months there, Megan backpacked her way through Argentina, Uruguay, Peru, Ecuador, and Colombia. She now works for the Carnegie Corporation of New York as a Program Analyst in the New Designs to Advance Learning portfolio and awaits her next great adventure in Latin America.

About the Editors

Karen Attman's writing has appeared in over twenty-five publications around the world, including CNN, Esquire, and Four Magazine. Her book on specialty coffee, *Permission to Slurp*, has been widely received by experts in the coffee industry and is required reading in university courses. Find out more about her at www.flavorsofbogota.com.

Victoria Kellaway was an award-winning newspaper reporter in England before she moved to Bogota, Colombia. She co-wrote the bestselling satire *Colombia a comedy of errors*, stocked by entities as diverse as the Harvard Library in Massachusetts, USA, and the Nobel Peace Center in Oslo, Norway. Find out more about Victoria at www.bananaskinflipflops.com.

Emma Newbery is the managing editor and co-founder of *The Bogotá Post*, Colombia's hard-hitting English-language newspaper, and co-founder of the boutique publishing house The Bogotá International Press. Emma began her working life as a financial journalist before helping to bring the Olympic Games to London. She then spent almost a decade advising cities that hope to host the world's largest sporting extravaganza.

Acknowledgements

We would like to thank all the women who entered the 2017 Women Travel Latin America Writing Competition and shared not only their stories but their hearts and souls in their contributions. Thank you to these inspiring women who made *Alone Together* possible.

We also want to thank our proofreaders and editors who reminded us to include those overlooked commas and helped ferret out those hidden typos. Our heartfelt thanks go to: Stacie Weddle, Mary Tracy, Lynda Newbery, and Sally Wilson.

Made in the USA
San Bernardino, CA
06 June 2019